MW00333533

How to Get a Teaching Job

How to Get a Teaching Job

Courtney W. Moffatt
Edgewood College

Thomas L. Moffatt
Management Dynamics, Inc.

INDIANAPOLIS MARION CO. PUBLIC LIBRARY

Allyn and Bacon

Boston ■ London ■ Toronto ■ Sydney ■ Tokyo ■ Singapore

Executive editor: *Stephen D. Dragin*
Series editorial assistant: *Bridget McSweeney*
Marketing manager: *Brad Parkins*
Manufacturing buyer: *David Repetto*

Copyright © 2000 by Allyn & Bacon
A Pearson Education Company
Needham Heights, MA 02494

Internet: www.abacon.com

All rights reserved. No part of the material protected by this copyright notice may be reproduced or utilized in any form or by any means, electronic or mechanical, including photocopying, recording, or by any information storage and retrieval system, without written permission from the copyright owner.

Between the time Website information is gathered and then published, it is not unusual for some sites to have closed. Also, the transcription of URLs can result in unintended typographical errors. The publisher would appreciate notification where these occur so that they may be corrected in subsequent editions. Thank you.

Library of Congress Cataloging-in-Publication Data

Moffatt, Courtney W.
    How to get a teaching job / Courtney W. Moffatt, Thomas L. Moffatt.
        p.   cm.
    Includes bibliographical references and index.
    ISBN 0-205-29924-5
    1. Teachers—Employment—United States Handbooks, manuals, etc.
2. Teaching—Vocational guidance—United States Handbooks, manuals, etc.   I. Moffatt, Thomas L.   II. Title.
LB1780.M64   2000
370'.23'73—dc21   99-42480
                                                                   CIP

Printed in the United States of America

10   9   8   7   6   5   4   3   2   1   03   02   01   00   99

We would like to dedicate this book to our family and especially to Rosalie Moffatt for all the patience and love she has shown us.

CONTENTS

PREFACE AND ACKNOWLEDGMENTS

This book is designed to be used by individuals in the field of education, or outside of it, to enhance their employability as professionals and their ability to find a match between their skills and the needs and assets of a school. Educators are encouraged to read the table of contents and then the individual chapter outlines and competencies in order to decide which information is applicable to their needs at the time. This book is designed to be a resource and reference and need not necessarily be read cover to cover.

Each competency is listed at the beginning of the chapter, along with the pages that further explore the competency. It is designed to meet some of the needs that a job hunter in education will encounter. If you are interested in the field of education and are just beginning school, if you are unemployed or underemployed, or if you are securely employed but sense that there could be a more satisfying job awaiting you, this book may provide the impetus or advice you need to keep going in the right direction.

The purpose of *How to Get a Teaching Job* is to explain not only where to look for a teaching job but also how to look for a job, how to identify it once you have found it, how best to present your qualifications to fill it, and what to do if all else fails. It investigates the mysteries of the job market—what goes on behind those closed doors where interviews are conducted.

This book was developed because both of us discovered, after presenting numerous job seminars, advising undergraduate and graduate students, and talking to teachers, principals, and superintendents, that individuals in the field of education often have very little understanding of the intricacies of finding the right job.

Ultimately, we realize that the desires of the interviewers and those of the applicants they interview are not so very different. Applicants don't want to feel fearful or defensive or forced to play games. And much of the unknown and "plastic" quality of the interviewing process could be eliminated if potential job applicants knew what to expect and how to prepare themselves for it. If job candidates know how the interviewing and employment process works in various schools and school districts, how best to assess their own qualifications and desires, and how to present their assets to the interviewer honestly and confidently, the chances are very good that such applicants will apply for the right jobs—those for which they are qualified and that they really want—and will sail through interviews with greater self-confidence. Thus the interviewer will get a truer picture of the applicant's actual qualifications and eventually hire the person best suited to the job. As a result, both applicant and interviewer will find the process less painful and more productive.

In closing, we would like to wish every reader an easy and fruitful job search, resulting in better self-understanding and a profitable and happy career. If the step-by-step instructions and tips in this book help to bring about that conclusion, then we will indeed feel that our efforts in writing *How to Get a Teaching Job* have been amply rewarded.

Our appreciation goes to Robert J. David, California University of Pennsylvania, for his helpful comments in reviewing the manuscript, Stephen D. Dragin, my executive editor, and Bridget McSweeney, series editorial assistant, for their interest, invaluable time, and assistance with this manuscript. Thank you also to Judy Ashkenaz, Project Manager at Stratford Publishing Services, Inc.

Courtney W. Moffatt
Thomas L. Moffatt

ABOUT THE AUTHORS

Courtney Moffatt is an associate professor in education at a private college in the Midwest. She speaks to educators across the country, writes extensively, and heads a special education graduate program. She is certified in elementary education K–8, learning disabilities K–12, emotional disturbance K–12, and cognitive disabilities K–12, and has experience teaching in all areas.

Thomas L. Moffatt teaches part time and has been president of Management Dynamics for thirty years. He has written many books, including *Land That Job!* and *Selection Interviewing,* and has thirty-five years' experience teaching interviewing skills.

Is Teaching Really for Me?

This chapter should help you think more deeply about what you want or how to explain to a potential employer what you want.

OUTLINE

COMPETENCIES COVERED IN CHAPTER 1

Part B. Where Is My Niche?

   1. How do different education occupations rank?

Part C. What Would I Need to Do to Be Able to Teach?

   1. What can I do if I decide I want a job in education and my undergraduate degree is not in teaching?

Part D. Help, I Don't Have Any Teaching Experience!

   1. As a parent returning to work I am unsure about how to sell myself.
   2. I am a recent graduate attempting to develop a resume and describe my experience, yet it may be difficult as I have not had any "real" jobs as yet.
   3. I am changing careers, moving into the field of education, and as yet unable to describe my situation in a positive light.

CASE STUDY

When Linda first came to our office, she had just updated her training and completed all state requirements for elementary education certification at the first through fifth grade level. However, as much as she was looking forward to teaching after her second child began first grade, she also realized that perhaps she wasn't ready to spend all day working with grade school children and come home to the same age group each night. She also had a creative bent that she felt was hard to express when working with very young children. She discovered through her literature courses that she was very excited about writing. However, she also realized that most of her grade school students, even in her fifth grade classes, would be unable to write with the complexity she so enjoyed. Only after some serious research into the entire field of education and some soul searching, did Linda come to the conclusion that for the next few years she might be happiest teaching writing at the high school level, necessitating a secondary English certification.

Fortunately, Linda was able to assess her situation honestly and alleviate her misgivings by completing her work in an English program the following year; this permitted her to acquire secondary English certification and procure a job by the following school year. She reports that she will be forever grateful that she spent the extra year gaining the necessary training to do something she so greatly enjoys.

Stories like these are not uncommon in the field of education. Teachers' interests can easily change over time or can conflict with present circumstances.

Since you are reading this book we will assume that you are interested in the teaching profession. This is a wonderful choice despite the gruesome reports you may have heard about the situation of schools across the country. Teaching is a wonderful way to achieve a sense of accomplishment and satisfaction from your work while participating in a worthwhile endeavor that can positively affect the future. However, you must obtain a position in order to accomplish your goals. Before you can be hired, you must decide what your preference is in the area of teaching. Besides evaluating your likes and dislikes, you must evaluate your strengths and weaknesses. After putting all of this together you are then ready to look further in the market and see where you might be most needed.

How to Use Inventories for Self-Appraisal Purposes

No matter what your age you can benefit from an objective look at your talents and interests. On occasion the area we choose as our professional goal may have more basis in our parents' expectations of us than what we might truly enjoy. From the time we were born our parents have probably had a vision of us, and this vision can easily cloud our reason. If you are curious about your own decisions about your future and think perhaps you would like to get another opinion, try going to your college campus testing center and finding what inventories they may recommend. There are many good inventories of career interests. Of particular value are the:

- Career Assessment Inventory
- Edwards Personal Preference Schedule
- Kuder Occupational Inventory
- Strong Interest Inventory®
- System of Interactive Guidance and Information Plus Program

Two of the best are the System of Interactive Guidance and Information Plus Program and the Strong Interest Inventory. Try taking a formal or informal inventory of your interests and you might be surprised.

Strong Interest Inventory

One helpful inventory might be the Strong Interest Inventory (Harmon, Hansen, Borgen, & Hammer, 1994). This test can be found in most college campus testing centers. Whether or not you decide to take this assessment, you may be interested in the basic classification system the authors investigated. By testing individuals employed in many different occupations, John Holland developed lists of interests of individuals by profession. This was accomplished in two ways, first by asking individuals to describe which characteristics were most like them, then by asking individuals of known types which occupations they liked. These interests were then grouped into six broad categories, described as general themes.

The Strong Interest Inventory's descriptions for these themes are as follows:

® The Strong Interest Inventory and SII are registered trademarks of Stanford University Press.

Realistic.   People who have high realistic scores like mechanical, construction, and repair activities. They enjoy working outdoors, adventure, and physical activities. They report enjoying working with their hands and tools to build things such as a radio or cabinets, and to fix things such as broken toys or furniture. These people prefer working alone or with one or two people rather than with a large group. They describe themselves as having good physical skills, as being practical and rugged, and as generally preferring to work with things, such as machines, rather than with people. They prefer occupations such as vocational agriculture teacher, industrial arts teacher, auto mechanic, plumber, electrician, police officer, engineer, farmer, military officer, forester, and park ranger. The word *realistic* has been used to describe this area. The typical work activities they report enjoying include:

- Doing jobs that produce tangible results
- Operating or designing heavy equipment or huge machines
- Using tools that require fine motor coordination and manual dexterity
- Operating precision machinery
- Fixing, building, and repairing

Investigative.   These people like activities and occupations that are related to science or mathematics, activities with an inquiring orientation. They enjoy gathering information and uncovering new facts and analyzing and interpreting data. They are most comfortable in academic or research environments. They prefer to rely on themselves rather than others in a group. They dislike selling and repetitive activities. They prefer occupations such as college professor, science teacher, physician, pharmacist, laboratory research worker, medical technician, chemist, computer programmer, optometrist, geologist, dentist, drafter, veterinarian, and medical technician. The word used to describe them is *investigative*. The typical work activities they report enjoying include:

- Performing ambiguous or abstract tasks
- Solving problems through thinking
- Working independently
- Doing scientific or laboratory work
- Conducting research and analysis
- Collecting and organizing data

Artistic.   People of this type value aesthetic qualities and have a great need for self-expression. They enjoy being spectators or observers rather than participants. They like to work in a job with many possibilities for expressing themselves by making and creating works of art. They also like to express their artistic interests in their leisure or recreational activities. They usually like to wrap themselves up in what they are doing. Generally, they like to do such things as writing poetry, drawing, or sketching. They are similar to investigative people in not liking to work where there are lots of rules. They are happier when what they create means something to them personally. They frequently describe themselves as imaginative, original, expressive, and artistic. Occupational choices include art teacher, English teacher, artist, author, cartoonist, musician, poet, actor/actress, broadcaster, advertising executive, newspaper reporter, photographer, librarian, and interior designer. *Artistic* is the word used to describe this theme area. The typical work activities they report enjoying include:

- Composing writing
- Creating artwork
- Working independently
- Acting, performing
- Playing musical instruments
- Decorating, designing

Social. People who have high scores on this scale tend to have a very strong concern for other people and like to help them solve personal problems. They prefer to solve problems by talking things out and they get along well with many types of people. They usually have little interest in working with machines and prefer doing activities that let them be helpful. They like working in groups, sharing responsibilities, and being the center of attention. They can frequently be described as helpful, nurturing, considerate, patient, and generous. Some occupations preferred by these people are elementary school teacher, home economics teacher, high school counselor, speech pathologist, occupational therapist, social worker, recreation leader, parks and recreation coordinator, camp counselor, agriculture extension agent, child care assistant, and public health nurse. The word *social* has been used to describe this area. The typical work activities they report enjoying include:

- Teaching, explaining
- Enlightening, guiding
- Helping, facilitating
- Selecting, training
- Informing, organizing
- Solving problems, leading discussions

Enterprising. People who have high scores on this scale are good at talking and using words to persuade and lead other people. Often they are in sales work and they are clever at thinking of new ways to do things that lead and convince people. They see themselves as full of energy, enthusiastic, adventurous, ambitious, competitive, outspoken, and confident. They seek positions of leadership, power, and status. They enjoy working with other people and frequently work in business. They strive to lead others toward organizational goals and economic success. Many times they are in occupations such as real estate salesperson, buyer/merchandiser, hotel manager, marketing executive, restaurant manager, purchasing agent, auctioneer, dental hygienist, advertising manager, insurance sales, and travel agent. The word *enterprising* describes these interests. The typical work activities they report enjoying include:

- Selling, purchasing
- Political maneuvering
- Entertaining clients
- Leading committees, groups, organizations
- Giving speeches, talks, and presentations
- Managing people and projects

Conventional.   These people prefer activities and jobs where they know exactly what is expected of them and what they are supposed to do. They work well in large organizations, but do not show a preference for or against leadership positions. They enjoy mathematics and data management activities such as accounting and investment that require attention to detail. Such people describe themselves as conventional, stable, well controlled, moderate, conforming, cautious, and dependable. They prefer jobs such as business education teacher, banker, actuary, bookkeeper, certified public accountant, credit manager, clerical worker, proofreader, computer operator, administrative assistant, and secretary. The word *conventional* has been used to describe these activities and jobs. The typical work activities they report enjoying include:

- Conducting a financial analysis
- Operating office machines
- Organizing office procedures
- Keeping records and financial books
- Writing business reports
- Making charts and graphs

Please note that these descriptions describe the people in different occupations as a group and may not fit any one person. Nor do they necessarily fit individual ability, only interests. This table is developed from the information in the *Strong Interest Inventory: Application and Technical Guide*. For further information, contact Consulting Psychologists Press, in Palo Alto, California. (Harmon, Hansen, Borgen, & Hammer, 1994). More information on the Strong Interest Inventory can also be obtained through their web site, www.cppdb.com, and CareerHub.org.

Teacher Themes

When looking at the Strong Interest Inventory Occupations and Theme codes it is interesting to note the different themes as they apply to different fields of education. For instance, you may note that elementary school teachers, social science teachers, and special education teachers all scored very high in the social area. However, female mathematics teachers have no social listing and

FIGURE 1.1.   1994 Strong Interest Inventory Occupations and Their Theme Codes

Teacher Themes

Occupation	Themes
Art teacher	AS
Business education teacher	CES
College professor	IA
Elementary teacher	S
English teacher	ASE
Home economics teacher	SE
Industrial arts teacher	RS
Physical education teacher	SR
Science teacher	IRS
Social science teacher	SEA
Special education teacher	SEA
Vocational agriculture teacher	RS

Key: R Realistic   S Social   I Investigative   A Artistic   C Conventional   E Enterprising

scored very high in the area of conventional, investigative, and realistic, as you can see in Figure 1.1.

Now that you have looked at some different teaching fields according to the theme specified, you may think a bit more about job descriptions and related job areas. Perhaps you are a female who finds you are strongest in the social theme followed by the enterprising and conventional. Since your profile points toward teaching home economics, often called family and consumer science, you might want to take a look at how The Education and Testing Service (ETS) describes the duties of a family and consumer science teacher in its career guidance and planning software, System of Interactive Guidance and Information (SIGIPLUS) Program (1998). It may be of further interest to you to note that consumer service consultant, extension service agent, 4-H Club agent, home economist, home extension agent, and home-service director are related fields that you could pursue in the future. (See Figure 1.2 for related job areas.)

As you look over the list, think of yourself and how you might fit into the themes as listed by the Strong Inventory. Do you think you fit into a theme? Do you agree with the occupational categories? Perhaps for you it might be useful to think of these themes as an indication of what type of person you might work with in an educational environment. If you have decided that you would love to be a college professor yet are very social and love to work with people and not science or numbers, you may be an excellent college professor but may find yourself very different from your colleagues.

FIGURE 1.2.   Education-Related Jobs

Business Education Teacher
Related Jobs
Accountant
Benefits analyst
Bookkeeping
Business law teacher
Computer programmer
Merchandising specialist

College Professor
Related Jobs
Dean
Department chair
Retirement counselor
School administration
Technical institute instructor

Early Childhood Teacher
Related Jobs
Children's television production
Day care coordinator
Head Start teacher

Elementary Teacher
Related Jobs
Children's author
Children's magazine editor
Children's tutor
Curriculum development
Day care worker
Kindergarten teacher
Nursery school teacher
Preschool teacher
Remedial teacher
Teacher's aide

English Teacher
Related Jobs
Columnist

Editor
Journalist
Literature teacher
Publicity advisor
Speech teacher
Speech writer
Writer
Writing teacher

Fine Arts Teacher
Related Jobs
   Art
Art therapist
Crafts instructor
Design instructor
Drawing teacher
Graphic artist
Industrial designer
   Music
Choir director
Conductor
Music studio
Private music teacher

Foreign Language Teacher
Related Jobs
Airline hostess
ESL/Bilingual teacher
International agency
Interpreter/Translator
Travel guide

**Family and Consumer
Science Teacher**
Related Jobs
Dietitian
Food service consultant
Food service director

FIGURE 1.2. Continued

Extension service agent
4-H Club agent
Home economist
Interior decorator
Restaurateur

Mathematics Teacher
Related Jobs
Accountant
Actuary
Auditor
Bookkeeper
Computational linguist
Computer science teacher
Statistician
Tax consultant
Trigonometry/Calculus
  teacher

Physical Education Teacher
Related Jobs
Aquatics director
Athletic director
Coach
Fitness center owner/ manager
Leisure consultant
Personal trainer
Referee

Science Teacher
Related Jobs
Astronomy teacher
Bionic electron technician
Earth science teacher
Ecologist
Geologist

Geology teacher
Health teacher
Horticulturist
Medical technician
Physiology teacher
Robot technician
Water quality scientist

Social Science Teacher
Related Jobs
American studies teacher
Career development
  advisor
Criminology teacher
Economics teacher
Museum guide
Parole officer
Political science teacher
Psychology teacher
Sociologist
Social worker
Urban planner

Special Education Teacher
Related Jobs
After-school tutorial service
Guidance counselor
Homebound instructor
Hospital instructor
Physical therapist
School psychologist
Social service agency
  caseworker
Social worker
Speech therapist
Transition specialist

Where Is My Niche?

Everyone wants to do well but if you are not in the right area, you may not achieve the same success you would achieve if you were in an area that was a better fit with your talents and skills. It is worth taking the time to at least think about this before embarking on a career that might not exactly suit you.

After appraising your interests and themes in contrast to others in your chosen area of interest, it is time to look at the different duties usually associated with different areas of teaching.

Review of the Teaching Profession

All areas of teaching include the following duties:

- Instructing students through classroom presentations, demonstrations, discussions, and group projects
- Preparing outlines for courses of study, designing goals and the content to meet these goals, and prioritizing concepts and skills to be learned
- Developing daily lesson plans to guide instruction and assessment devices such as homework, performance-based tests, and quizzes to assess students' progress toward attainment of instructional goals
- Developing practical assignments and lessons to connect information to concepts in the real world
- Correcting student homework and using students' assigned work to evaluate and adapt future lessons
- Keeping a record of student attendance and maintaining discipline
- Participating in faculty and professional meetings, conferences, and teacher-training workshops
- Performing duties related to students' life in the school and community, for example by sponsoring special activities and student organizations
- Acting as liaison with parents and public

Perhaps the career information found in ETS's SIGIPLUS software, which provides a review of more specific roles and responsibilities of the different teaching areas, will be helpful to your self-evaluation. The following information on teachers' roles and responsibilities is taken from the SIGIPLUS program.

Business Education Teacher
A teacher in business education teaches mostly secondary students courses in business English, business law, bookkeeping, accounting, economics, computer applications, shorthand, marketing, merchandising, information/word processing,

---

Source: The source for much of the information provided here is the SIGIPLUS program, a product of Educational Testing Service. Used by permission.

and office management. These courses are taught to help prepare students for careers in business and office support and to give helpful skills to other students who may not be looking for a career in business but have need of the skills. Teachers may also work in elementary and middle schools developing computer application programs.

College Professor

A college professor conducts college or university classes for undergraduate or graduate students. This individual prepares and delivers lectures, facilitates and stimulates discussions, and directs students to further areas of research. The professor compiles, administers, and grades examinations or assigns this work to others. Professors might also direct the research of others, particularly when involved with graduate education. College professors usually conduct research in particular fields of knowledge and then present their findings at professional meetings and publish them in professional journals. They perform related duties such as advising students, working with student organizations, and serving on faculty committees. College professors are often deeply involved in undergraduate and graduate program development and assessment and in preparing materials for professional program review and certification.

Early Childhood Teacher

Early childhood teachers generally work with children from birth to five years of age. These programs are usually in the public schools but may also be run by individuals in the private sector for profit. Programs range from ten months a year for a few hours a day, a few days a week, to twelve hours a day year-round. Early childhood teachers plan and supervise activities to meet each child's developmental needs in social, academic, speech, and motor areas of development. Early childhood teachers are often responsible for building rapport with parents and encouraging positive family–school collaboration. Some early childhood teachers are involved in parent training.

Elementary Teacher

An elementary school teacher usually has a class of 15 to 30 elementary school students in one grade from kindergarten to fifth or sixth grade. This individual is usually responsible for teaching all academic subjects to students in their assigned class. The elementary school teacher may be involved in team teaching with other teachers at the same grade level in the school or perhaps team teaching with a special education teacher. Academic subject areas of responsibility usually include but are not limited to: reading, writing, arithmetic, science, and social studies. Generally the regular education teacher is also responsible for fostering personal growth and teaching children social and study skills such as staying in their seats, not bothering others, following directions, and practicing good citizenship. Elementary school teachers demonstrate and use multiple computer and audiovisual teaching aids to present subject matter. They prepare, administer, and correct tests; assign lessons; and correct papers. Elementary teachers counsel students when adjustment, academic, or behavioral problems arise; often, they discuss these problems with a child's parents and suggest remedial action. Elementary teachers are responsible for keeping attendance and grade records as required by their school board.

English Teacher

English teachers teach courses in language arts such as reading, composition, literature, grammar, poetry, creative writing, and speech. They teach in middle and secondary schools in the public or private sector. They teach students the rules of English grammar and usage, they teach literature understanding and appreciation, and they facilitate and improve students' ability to write for different purposes and for various audiences. They also teach students communication skills such as listening, speaking, and performing.

ESL/Bilingual Teacher

Bilingual teachers or English as a second language (ESL) teachers work with students who speak another language. They usually teach their students reading, writing, and speaking English, often not using the students' native languages. (The ESL teacher often will not know the students' languages.) Bilingual teachers primarily teach language but they may also be involved in teaching their students other academic areas such as mathematics, social studies, and science until the students have enough English to profit from regular classroom instruction. ESL teachers may teach at any level from preschool to adult. They are most often hired to teach in the K–12 schools but also work in higher education and adult education programs. They can also teach in private language schools where only English is taught.

Fine Arts Teacher

Fine arts teachers instruct K–12 students in aesthetics, art production, art history, and art appreciation. They teach courses in skills such as drawing, computer graphics, photography, painting, sculpture, weaving, jewelry design and production, and filmmaking. Skills in how to use color, perspective, 3-D design, and appreciation for art throughout history and into the present are often also part of the curriculum.

Foreign Language Teacher

Teaching courses in grammar, reading, and the speaking of various languages plus cultural customs, history, geography, and literature are all possible areas of instruction for foreign language teachers. They often teach students about other languages by using the language in class, as the primary communication device. In these classes, students often have the opportunity to converse with each other and write in the foreign language, as well as to sing songs and read literature from that language and culture.

Family and Consumer Science Teacher

Teachers in the area of family and consumer science teach courses involved in daily family care. They often teach specialized courses in foods, diet, and nutrition; textiles and apparel; budget management and family economics; human development and child care; and living environments and interior design. They usually teach in middle schools and/or high schools in the public and private sector. In middle schools they usually will teach a required course to all students, male and female, at a certain grade level, which will include general information in all areas of family and daily living skills. They also will teach more specific courses, especially at the high school level, in one of the aforementioned areas to interested students who elect to take further training in a specialized field.

Mathematics Teacher

A mathematics teacher teaches courses such as algebra, geometry, calculus, general mathematics, consumer mathematics, and computer science. Throughout all instruction, the teacher demonstrates the use of mathematical theory as well as the practical use of mathematics in everyday living. A few teach in elementary schools that have specialists teaching science (rather than the regular education teacher), however licensing must cover the K–5 grade level in order to work with this population.

Physical Education Teacher

Physical education teachers instruct students in physical education activities usually in the K–12 system. They often, especially at grade levels above third grade, teach field, court, and combative sports to individuals or groups, using their knowledge of sports techniques and of the physical capabilities of their students. They also instruct individuals or groups in fitness, calisthenics, aquatics, dance, and gymnastics. Physical education teachers also may teach corrective exercises and determine the type and level of difficulty of exercise needed by each student, so as to help the student develop appropriate technique and movement. They organize, lead, instruct, and referee indoor and outdoor games.

Science Teacher

A science teacher instructs students in the areas of science, such as earth and space science, physics, biology, botany, and chemistry, usually at the middle or high school level. The instructor leads classroom presentations, organizes group investigations and lab experiments, teaches safety rules, leads dissections, and instructs students in the methods of scientific investigation and inquiry, including deductive reasoning, collection, organization, and analysis of data.

Social Studies Teacher

A social studies or social science teacher teaches courses such as American studies, career exploration, economics, geography, government, civics, history, and political science in middle schools, junior highs, or high schools. In some schools, courses also may be offered in religious studies, psychology, philosophy, anthropology, women's studies, or ethnic studies. Social studies teachers are usually involved in teaching students to critically analyze textbook readings and to use the resources of the school instructional resource center and public libraries. They teach important concepts through simulation, cooperative group work, multimedia presentations, and community, state, national, and—on rare occasions—even international field trips.

Special Education Teacher

Special education teachers are responsible for working with individuals who have been determined to have disabilities. Students' ages may range from infancy to young adult. Special education teachers adapt teaching techniques and material to the needs defined in each student's individual educational plan in order to help students reach their maximum potential. Special education teachers may teach in their own classrooms, teach their students in the special education classroom a few hours a day, or teach collaboratively and cooperatively with regular education teachers throughout the day. Most special education teachers cover a variety of these roles, depending on the needs of each of their students. It is most common for special education teachers to be placed on a team developed for the purpose of testing and evaluating a student's individual needs, as well as determining initial placement and continued placement or withdrawal from special education services. Special education teachers are also responsible, along with parents and key individuals, for planning students' transitions into the community and workforce after graduation. Special education teachers are often assigned to the students that they serve throughout the student's placement in a school.

Technology Education Teacher

Technology education teachers run programs to help students become technologically literate in grades 6 through 12. They teach courses in technology, in the areas of construction, manufacturing, energy, and power. Students learn how to solve problems using a variety of tools and techniques, including mathematics and science. Technology education teachers must teach and enforce student safety standards in the use of power tools.

What Would I Need to Do to Be Able to Teach?

In the past, individuals graduated from two-year teacher colleges in order to become teachers. Today, all fifty states require teachers to hold valid teaching certificates issued by their state departments of public instruction and certification. Almost all states also require a bachelor's degree and student teaching before becoming certified. Therefore, if you are interested in teaching, you should begin by entering a college or university that offers a program in education. Next, you will probably begin your program by fulfilling general degree requirements and taking courses such as history and English. In your sophomore or junior year, you would probably begin taking courses in the education department. At many colleges and universities students must apply and be accepted into the education department of their school before they can enter. Once in the education department they usually choose an area of concentration or major within the field. At this time students decide whether they are interested in elementary education, middle or secondary education, or perhaps early childhood, kindergarten, or special education. From here they often narrow their focus even further, such as middle school math/science, high school Spanish, or K-8 learning disabilities. The best way to make your choice, which is probably the best way to make any choice, is by gathering information so as to make a well-informed decision. Talk with teachers in many different fields, and study the pros and cons of the area as they relate to you. Learn about the opportunities for employment in the area at this time and for the future. And, most important, see for yourself! Spend time in classrooms whenever you can, and volunteer to work in those classrooms that most spark your interest. Even if you are still in high school, many high schools offer students the opportunity to work in middle and grade school classrooms so as to learn more about the teaching profession. Then question yourself about what you like/dislike and why. Keep a journal as you volunteer in different classrooms so that you have a record of your experience to review with other experiences in the classroom at later dates. This will help you analyze yourself and your decision to teach. At the end of each volunteer experience, you can rate the experience according to your preference from one (least) to five (most) preferred (see the Experience Comparison Chart, Figure 1.3). If you find your experiences very difficult to rate, you can count your pros and subtract your cons for a numerical rating. This should help you see a pattern so that you can visually compare your experiences at different levels in different settings with varying types of students.

FIGURE 1.3. Experience Comparison Chart

1. Experience

LEAST	1	2	3	4	5	MOST

Liked_____ Disliked _____

2. Experience

LEAST	1	2	3	4	5	MOST

Liked_____ Disliked _____

3. Experience

LEAST	1	2	3	4	5	MOST

Liked_____ Disliked _____

(continued)

FIGURE 1.3.   (continued)

---

4. Experience

LEAST	1	2	3	4	5	MOST

Liked_____ Disliked _____

5. Experience

LEAST	1	2	3	4	5	MOST

Liked_____ Disliked _____

6. Experience

LEAST	1	2	3	4	5	MOST

Liked_____ Disliked _____

7. Experience

LEAST	1	2	3	4	5	MOST

Liked_____ Disliked _____

8. Experience

LEAST	1	2	3	4	5	MOST

Liked_____ Disliked _____

9. Experience

LEAST	1	2	3	4	5	MOST

Liked_____ Disliked _____

Many colleges and universities require that their education students take a standardized test, usually in the sophomore or junior year. Frequently, this is a national test required by the State Department of Public Instruction that evaluates students' proficiency in reading, math, and writing. Some colleges and universities add other examinations as well that require the students to demonstrate their ability in spelling, handwriting, and phonics. This may be part of the students' development of a teaching portfolio, wherein students gather materials to demonstrate their skills and abilities in the area of instruction and knowledge of their field.

Teacher training at the undergraduate level frequently includes multiple practicum experiences giving students the opportunity to try newly acquired skills in the school setting before the final semester, which is usually the culminating experience of student teaching. By this time, it is hoped that students will have the information to choose the subject and level in which they most want to teach. However, no matter how many courses and volunteer experiences a student acquires, nothing is like an actual student-teaching experience to help an individual choose more closely the area in which they want to teach. Remember to study all the areas available to you carefully so that you can think about the one that most interests you.

Teachers majoring in elementary education are usually required to follow a liberal studies program along with courses in methods of teaching in each area of the curriculum, frequently including reading methods, math methods, language arts methods, and science/social methods.

High school teachers usually take most of their course work in their field of specialization, be it mathematics, science, English, foreign language, art, business education, agriculture, computers, or family and consumer science. Courses in the school of education are also required but the area of specialization takes precedent. In many states these specialization areas are broken down into very specific areas such as choral music or band, French or Spanish, learning or cognitive disabilities.

The student teaching experience usually involves full-time teaching for at least eight weeks. The minimum amount of time required is determined by each state's department of instruction, which is responsible for teacher licensure and specifying when the student teacher must be supervised by a teacher and a university supervisor.

Once a student finishes all of the requirements for licensure, their college or university will recommend them for certification. This recommendation is sent to the State Department of Public Instruction and Certification, and that body then issues a temporary or probationary license.

What If My Bachelor's Degree Is Not in Teaching?

In many states, but not all, your educational background or college major is becoming less important as job opportunities in the field of teaching increase. Many state departments of public instruction, in conjunction with college education departments, are developing fast-track programs to train and certify teachers quickly, whether or not their undergraduate degrees or experience have been in the field of education. The baby boomers and children of baby boomers are increasing the need for teachers at the elementary, middle, and high school levels. The number of children in United States schools should top 54 million by 2001, according to George Thompson in "Teaching Boom: A Surprising Solution to the Career Puzzle," in the magazine *Managing Your Career*, published by the *Wall Street Journal* (Spring–Summer 1995). Especially hot areas of need are in the fields of bilingual education, special education, science, and math. Geographically, educators will find their services particularly in demand in rural areas and extremely populated urban areas. Your prospects look continually brighter.

Help, I Don't Have Any Teaching Experience!

Although the second chapter will provide most education applicants with help in taking stock to put together a resume, there will invariably be some who still just cannot think of how to go about it. The big difficulty here usually lies in the fact that the applicant has not been working (in fact, may never have worked) or does not perceive past work experience as relevant to the kind of job now being sought. A resume is rarely a problem for the person who has done a particular type of work for some time and who hopes to continue to do exactly the same things only at a higher salary or perhaps in a different location. However, this knowledge is not very comforting to those who find themselves groping for a completely new career, so we will devote a few pages here to these applicants' special problems.

The Parent Returns to Work

It has been our experience that many people who have stayed home from work to manage a home and raise a family have amassed a wider variety of useful experience than those who are working outside of the home. However they often do not capitalize on these experiences when applying for a job. This is largely because they are not marketing their assets properly and are not thinking in terms of abilities they may have that would be an asset to the hiring organization.

The problem is that these bright and competent individuals, when faced with a return to the job market, often see themselves as "inexperienced." True, they may have little or no salary history or no paid experience. But they have plenty of experience. If you are an individual about to return to the workforce, then the key to self-appraisal is to think in terms of the skills you have, even if you never received a cent for performing them. Do you shine at organizing everything, teach scuba diving on the weekends, and coordinate your children's multiple activities before and after school? Put it on your resume. These are all assets that may be directly related to teaching.

Even more skills and talents surface if you add the skills and experience you have acquired through hobbies, organizations, volunteer activities, and other forms of participation outside the home. Maybe you were very active in the Parent Teacher Association (PTA or PTSO), publicity director of the local symphony orchestra, organizer of the city soccer league, or director of the local hospital's fund-raising drive. If you organized the European trip for the high school band, that is valuable community service. When entering these various skills and types of experience on your resume, be as specific as possible about what you accomplished. Examples:

- Organized The Child Exchange in 1997 with three other parents of preschoolers.
- Developed The Child Exchange as a cooperative babysitting service that lets parents earn hours away from their own children by sitting with the children of others.

- Coordinated The Child Exchange as a cooperative child care service with the children of others. By 1998, The Child Exchange had 119 parents as members and had established an executive committee to control its operation.
- Served as chairman of the executive committee of The Child Exchange from 1998 to present; kept track of hours served and owed for all member parents; appeared on local radio and television and wrote newspaper articles that were responsible for publicizing the organization and increasing membership.
- Helped interested individuals establish similar groups in other cities in three states.

If you have had job experience in the past, by all means include this on your resume even if many years have passed. However, it will be very helpful if you can demonstrate that you have worked at keeping your skills and knowledge in your field current.

If you have a degree in education that is not current, but are eager to take courses on your own so as to catch up, say so on your resume. Even better, enroll in a related class or two before submitting the resume. Briefly outline how you intend to continue once you are employed. You will be amazed at the number of employers who appreciate this sort of initiative and drive.

TIP Everyone has experience at something. *Never* write on your resume, "No experience."

The Recent Graduate

New graduates and individuals returning to work after an absence from the workforce have similar problems in devising a resume. New graduates suffer many of the same maladies as parents or individuals returning to work after a lengthy absence when they attempt to devise a resume. Quite naturally, they tend to think mainly in terms of their most current task, getting that diploma or degree while maintaining a respectable grade point average. But you are probably doing so much more at the same time. One of the most important jobs you will hold while in school is your semester of student teaching. The skills you learn on the job here will affect your teaching for the rest of your life. Be sure you capitalize on the skills you used on this most important job.

If you are a student about to leave school and embark on your career, you will have to do some creative thinking to come up with a self-appraisal and resume. A place to start could be with your part-time job experiences, however unrelated to education they may appear. Many young graduates hesitate to list these jobs, thinking their prospective employer will consider them insufficient. On the contrary, most employers understand that students today are often forced to take the part-time jobs that nobody else wants. Furthermore, they actually admire students who can show that (1) they have gained a wide variety of experience, as a result of part-time and summer work or (2) they have had the perseverance to stick with the same job throughout their years of schooling in order to reach a higher goal (securing enough income to stay in school).

Here again, list accomplishments, not duties, even though you may have to stretch your imagination to find any. If you worked in a grocery, you could estimate the number of customers you served per week and list the positions you held as you moved up within the organization, from bagger to cash register clerk. If you were a night guard at a warehouse for four years, during which there was not a single break-in, and you did not miss a single night of work, state this proudly. Day care, office work, and fast food manager all involve skills and accomplishments you can relate to teaching. If you can point to good attendance records, promotions, or additional responsibilities that were given to you, so much the better. You are really fortunate if you participated in work-study programs or landed a part-time job in a field related to the area in education in which you wish to teach.

Do not forget your participation in extracurricular activities during your school years, either. Even duties that you took on strictly for the fun of it may have given you the experience that will look valuable and demonstrate your versatility to an interviewer. Were you an officer in your fraternity, treasurer of your senior class, a writer for the school paper, or manager of the softball team? Employers look for these types of experiences, since they demonstrate your leadership, popularity, organizational ability, or just plain willingness to work behind the scenes for something that interests you. Persons who get along well with others and volunteer their time are an asset to any school.

If you have received honors in connection with your schooling or extracurricular activities, list these also. Membership in an honorary scholastic or professional society is always a good credential; so is being named "most likely to succeed" or "best citizen" by the high school yearbook staff. Honors earned through 4-H, scouting, Future Farmers of America (FFA), and similar youth organizations should be mentioned.

Now, examine your hobbies and the things you do at home. Soon, you'll have a self-assessment and a resume that shows you skills and preferences you never knew you had! Who knows, maybe you will even decide you have been in the wrong major all these years and really want to be a carpenter instead of a teacher!

In writing the resume, it is considered absolutely proper for new graduates to add a category called Career Goals, stating in general terms the way in which their educational background and skills might be put to use. This is especially true for the student who had a double major (e.g., business education and science education). Most prospective employers will be impressed to see that you have done some thinking about your career goals and have chosen a course of study to prepare yourself for them. A word of warning, though: Do not be so specific here that you cut yourself out of consideration for 90 percent of the jobs in your field. And do not be unrealistic about your capabilities. Also, most principals may not be eager to higher a business teacher whose stated goal is moving into a principalship in the next two to three years. We recommend that you leave this goal out.

TIP You may want to ask those close to you to look at your abilities and see if they see them as you do.

Changing Careers

If you are a mature, experienced individual who is considering a major change in careers, you will need to devote more time to self-appraisal. It is not terribly unusual today to encounter people who have had three or four successful careers during a typical forty-year work life. Some of these career changes are made from necessity, because certain skills have become obsolete and certain companies have closed their doors. Other changes are made strictly because personal choice or ambition have dictated that a change is in order. Whatever your reason, you are about to enrich your life with new experiences. Abundant educational opportunities and multiple economic and societal changes have presented almost unlimited opportunities for those who are energetic and talented enough to profit from them. We work with many excellent adults who are returning to school to develop their interests in teaching, and we find them a great asset to our programs and to all of the students and faculty with whom they come in contact. Their breadth of experience encourages us all to see teaching in a new way.

However, before contemplating such a career change you need to do some serious soul searching during the self-appraisal process. Most other job hunters need only ask themselves, "What skills do I have and how will I market them?" Career-changers must first ask themselves, "Do I really wish to make a change? If so, why? And what skills will I need to develop that I don't already have?"

A careful assessment and examination of your career goals for the next few years is in order. Why do you wish to change careers and what, specifically, do you hope to gain from such a change? Self-fulfillment or challenge? Relief from present boredom? Write down these answers, perhaps listing the things you hope to gain in one column and those you hope to escape in another. Be sure you know what your own personal goals and motives are before proceeding (see the Changing Jobs worksheet, Figure 1.4).

FIGURE 1.4. Changing Jobs

What I Hope to Gain	What I Hope to Escape

(continued)

FIGURE 1.4.   **(continued)**

Skills Needed

Time	Money

What are your present qualifications for teaching? List specific skills and personal characteristics you already possess that would transfer to the teaching field. Why do you think you could be successful in this field? What doubts do you have about your potential for success?

Next, inventory the skills you still need to acquire. This may take considerable research. Talk to people who are already successful in the teaching field of your choice; find out what skills and personal attributes they consider essential for "making it" in that area. Consider carefully whether you are lacking only some basic skills that could be acquired through education or training or whether you also lack important personal characteristics that cannot be readily acquired.

Finally, analyze the sacrifices you may have to make in order to change careers. What type of education will you need? How long will it take and what will it cost? Will you be able to take the necessary courses in your spare time, while retaining your current job? What financial risks will be involved? Will you have to give up vacations or evenings in order to take a part-time job so as to gain practical experience in the new field?

If you have carefully considered this important move over a period of time and are convinced that a major career change is in order, you will want to begin preparing yourself for this new venture. Read all you can about teaching, talk to others already engaged in education, and begin to get the training and additional formal education you need. If you need part-time experience before you feel qualified to apply for a full-time job in the new field, start getting it—even if you have to begin during vacations.

Because you do not wish to continue doing exactly what you were doing before, you will need to take great care in preparing your resume. List your former positions and accomplishments, emphasizing those skills and accomplishments that have the most bearing on the new educational field you are entering. You will want to place heavy emphasis on any training, courses, or part-time experience geared toward preparing you for the new endeavor. A brief section on career goals and/or a cover letter dealing with that topic is also in order. Here, you should explain in a positive manner your reasons for wishing to change careers, your conviction that this is the direction in which you want your life to move, and the steps you have taken to prepare yourself for this change. Negative reasons (e.g., "My job was boring," "My boss replaced me with a friend") should be rejected in favor of positive reasons that display your strong motivation to succeed in this new field and your belief that you have assets to offer a prospective employer.

TIP   Before changing careers:

1. List specific skills and personal characteristics that would make you a good teacher.
2. Inventory the skills you need to acquire.
3. Analyze what it will cost you in money and time.

This is an exciting time. Stay positive and enjoy it!

2 Starting the Search

This chapter deals with finding an appropriate teaching position.

OUTLINE

COMPETENCIES COVERED IN CHAPTER 2

Part A.   Start Early

1. When and how do I start looking for a job?
2. How can I ensure districts have "heard" of me?

Part B.   What Are Schools Looking For?

1. I want to know what school districts are looking for in teacher candidates.

2. I want to do a thorough self-evaluation, including things such as mental capabilities.
3. I would like to try charting this information to make it easier to use.
4. I want to list the qualities I have and don't have that will affect my ability to be effective in different educational settings.
5. I would like to list what I want and don't want in a job, in a clear and concise manner.

Part C. Packaging Your Military Experience for a Position in Education

1. How can I package my military experience in order to display its positive effect on a teaching position?

CASE STUDY

Adam always wanted to be a teacher, he loved kids and knew he had the best chance to make a difference in the world by giving young people the courage and convictions to behave responsibly.

He spent eighteen months in Colombia in mission work after finishing his college education. He then felt ready to make changes here at home. He got a job after his first interview in Texas in an innovative district with an outstanding grade school principal who proved to feel the same way he did about empowering children. Life was challenging and exhilarating.

Unfortunately, after Adam had been teaching in this school for eight years, things changed drastically. The economy took a nosedive and the school board decided to make major cutbacks. Suddenly neighborhood schools were closing and classrooms were bulging with an average of thirty-five students. The principal he so admired resigned in protest and his next two years were mired in teacher slowdowns and pending strikes.

He found himself so bogged down in politics that he was no longer able to enjoy his students, who had always been the joy of his life.

Only when he ran into an old friend he had known in the missionary did he realize just how much his attitude had changed about his work. He was constantly frustrated and no longer excited about going to work. He clearly needed to make a change. It was time for Adam to move on, although two years ago he would not have dreamed he would be feeling this way.

1. Have you ever noticed how life can change very unexpectedly? What changes might affect your happiness on the job?
2. Do you keep your options open so that you will always have a backup should a change occur in your situation? Try to list what you could do if you found you needed to completely change your life tomorrow.
3. List what more you could do to give yourself more options.

The good news for you if you find yourself searching for a job in education is that the field is opening up. This is especially true if you have more than one area of interest and licensure. Even in districts where new positions are not being created, teachers are retiring, quitting, moving, and being promoted. Therefore, there should be more possibilities for employment in the education field. The key is knowing where and how to look.

Start Early

When students ask us when they should begin looking for a teaching job, we always want to say, yesterday. Instead we want to limit their panic and say, "Immediately!"

You should always have your eyes and ears open for information about your field. Listen to any talk you hear on the subject of education, teaching, school districts, school boards, principals, and administrators. Even if you feel you have the best job in the world and you cannot imagine ever leaving, things can change overnight and the wise individual is always prepared.

Get Around and Be Known

Remember not to expend all your energy on your course work, although it is important to keep up your grade point average. You must not ignore your responsibility to yourself to begin your job search early. You should be signing up with credential services *before* your last semester of school. Get around and be known. It is also important that you familiarize yourself with school districts in which you might want to work. Introduce yourself wherever you go. Let people know that you are job searching. Make as many direct contacts as you can. There are probably teachers in your weight-lifting class or at your church who know about possible openings. You must be visible to teachers who already have jobs.

TIPS   Don't wait until you are done with school because, unfortunately, that other person sitting next to you in class probably will not wait.

Talk with friends and professors who may be able to assist you in finding job leads.

What Are Schools Looking For?

It is becoming increasingly obvious that the United States is very concerned about the state of its schools and the quality of teaching. Each year the need for teachers is predicted to rise steadily. The students filling these classrooms promise to be the most racially and ethnically diverse in history, thereby challenging the field to change to meet differing needs.

Teachers of the future must be knowledgeable about academic content, working with other educators, inclusion, and meeting the developmental needs of all students no matter what their home situations or what challenges they pose. Smart school districts are looking for individuals who can rise to this difficult task.

Instead of thinking like a teacher, we want you to think like a principal, superintendent of schools, and/or a school district personnel director. If you were in any of these positions, you would face certain problems every day. Think about what these problem might be. For example, as a grade school principal you have parents complaining because their child is in a large classroom and doesn't seem to be learning as well as expected. Or as the superintendent of schools, you have a problem of not enough space for all the classrooms and students you have. Perhaps you are the district personnel director, and the high school principal wants you to find someone capable of running health and wellness programs or student assistance teams, or the middle school principal needs a part-time language arts teacher.

If you, as a prospective teacher, understood the needs of the school district, perhaps you could help them solve their problems. Let us say you are a grade school teacher; perhaps you would be interested in helping the district apply for a grant to fund an at-risk program in which students who do not qualify for special education can receive extra help.

Remember the superintendent with the space problem? You might be the teacher who volunteers to have a classroom where the regular students and learning-disabled students share one big room between them, thereby gaining two teachers in one room and increasing building space.

If you had interest or training in alcohol- and other drug-abuse prevention (AODA), perhaps you could teach middle school language arts for half of each day and work at the high school in a health and wellness program the other half.

Remember, being flexible and willing to meet a district's needs through ingenuity, and perhaps pursuing further training, may make you the perfect and only viable candidate for the job.

TIPS   You must learn to think like a principal or school superintendent and keep the entire district's and/or school's needs in mind when you consider how you could be an asset to them.

The more training you have (e.g., AODA, SAP, or special education collaboration training) the more you will be assisted in finding the right teaching position.

In 1990 Gene Parker, director of Career Planning and Placement at West Texas State University, surveyed school districts to determine what characteristics they most desired in new teachers. School administrators, parents, and students all took part in this survey. Their top ten responses were summarized by the Association for School, College, and University Staffing, Inc., in their 1992 *Job Search Handbook for Educators* as follows.

Characteristics That School Systems Value

According to a report by Gene Parker, Director, Career Planning and Placement West Texas State University:

In 1990, our office surveyed school districts across the country to determine what characteristics were most desired in new teachers. School administrators, teachers, parents, and students took part in this survey, and the top ten responses are summarized here.

1. *The Ability to Make a Difference in a Student's Life*
   All those who are involved with school systems want teachers in their classrooms who sincerely like children and who are willing to work to see those children succeed.

2. *A Variety of Life Experiences*
   School systems look for teachers who bring with them a variety of experiences. Recent graduates whose resumes include volunteer work, camp counseling, and community work strike a responsive chord in the hiring office.

3. *Managing a Classroom*
   If you haven't taken a course in classroom management, you probably should, because school administrators are looking for evidence that you understand the task.

4. *Student Teaching Experiences*
   Administrators place strong emphasis on the evaluations you receive from your student teaching experience, so make the most of it.

5. *Academic Preparation*
   New certification requirements in nearly every state place increased emphasis on strong academic preparation.

6. *Personal Appearance*
   Like it or not, first impressions are important. Teacher candidates must present a professional appearance for interviews.

7. *A Sense of Humor*
   New teachers need to be able to laugh at situations and at themselves, recognizing that they are human and can make mistakes, just as students do.

8. *Adaptability*
   Administrators seek teachers who are able to bend, but not break. They look for assurance that you have demonstrated that you can withstand the pressures of the job.

9. *Maturity*
   Accountability and evaluation are increasingly important to school systems. Administrators want teachers who are able to withstand scrutiny and take criticism.

10. *Involvement*
    Teachers are expected to be active and assume leadership roles in the community. Administrators look for teachers who are willing to come in

early and stay late and who are dedicated to children. If you can make the most of the characteristics valued by the school system, your chances of being interviewed and chosen for a job will be greatly increased *(The Job Search Handbook for Educators).*

TIPS   As a principal, one of the things that will frustrate me the most is if you cannot manage your classroom. I would like to be reassured that if I hire you, you will be able to handle the classroom I give you.

Classroom management is important; educators agree that before learning can occur, the teacher must be in control of his or her classroom.

Self-Appraisal

As its name implies, the self-appraisal is performed just for you. Thus, no benefit is to be derived from dabbling in untruths, half-truths, or exaggerations. It is the best policy to be honest throughout the employment search and interview process; it is especially imperative to be agonizingly truthful with yourself during this appraisal phase.

Begin your self-appraisal by dividing a sheet of paper in half lengthwise to make a chart. Then, on one side, list your assets or pluses; on the other, list your corresponding liabilities or minuses. Take your time, be thorough, and—again—be honest. There is an advantage to not selling yourself short here, so if you have a tendency toward humility or self-effacement, try to think as positively as possible. By the same token, if you tend to have a pretty high opinion of yourself and your abilities, you should try not to overstate your qualifications or characteristics.

Although there is not a set format for the self-appraisal, since it is merely a personal worksheet, it will prove more useful to you if you organize the material in some meaningful fashion—either chronologically, by category, or in any other way that will make sense. As you begin listing your liabilities and assets, some sort of logical order will no doubt suggest itself to you (see Figure 2.1).

FIGURE 2.1.   Beginning My Self-Appraisal

Assets	Liabilities

Once you have completed a general appraisal of your assets and liabilities, you can begin the worksheet (Figure 2.2) in which you group these assets into specific areas, making them easier to sell to your future employer.

FIGURE 2.2. Self-Appraisal Worksheet

1. Education and Degrees

2. Other Educational Experiences

3. Work Experience

4. Volunteer Work

5. Personal Characteristics

6. Mental Capabilities

7. Physical Capabilities

8. Flexibility

The specific kinds of things that should be listed include:

- *Education and Degrees*
  In this section you can list all the courses and degrees from high school, college, junior college, technical schools, and so forth. These are, of course, great assets and you may want to highlight those you want to place most prominently. If you do not have a teaching license in your area of interest or if your degree was acquired many years ago and you haven't kept up with developments in your field, these are liabilities.

- *Other Educational Experience*
  Here you might include any educational experiences, such as those acquired in the military, the Peace Corps, job-related training provided by previous employers, extension courses, or seminars you've attended on your own. These need not have been for credit as long as you learned something that might prove useful to you in the future because it either broadened your knowledge or developed a particular skill. (Again, highlight those you want to stress.)

- *Work Experience*
  Under work experience, we would include not only the names of employers and the titles of jobs you have held but also the specific skills you were required to use on the job. Include supervisory or administrative skills as well as technical skills; types of equipment you operated; peripheral tasks you did as well as those that were an integral part of your job. Don't overlook part-time jobs, summer work, internships, or co-op programs, especially if you are heavy on education and light on work experience. Often the skills obtained in such interim jobs may seem to have little to do with your current career objectives or your major field of study, but an interviewer may see in them the little extra that qualifies you for a job or demonstrates your flexibility. In the work experience category, liabilities include lack of work experience, a poor work record, or the absence of a particular skill that would greatly enhance your chances for employment in your area of teaching.

  If you are a new teacher without any paid teaching experience, or a relatively new teacher with very little teaching experience, it can be very helpful to list all of your student teaching and even practicum placements. This is excellent "work experience" and should not be overlooked.

- *Volunteer Activities*
  You can acquire an amazing amount of skill and experience through time donated to special causes and volunteer activities. While doing an activity for the sake of enjoyment, rather than for a weekly paycheck, you are gaining invaluable skills and often developing something special within yourself. Almost every conceivable skill that constitutes one person's job constitutes another's volunteer activity, but all too often job seekers list only the skills they have previously been paid to use. Many valuable

skills may be acquired or improved upon during your donated time. These activities, no matter what or who they involve, may lead to the growth of your skills as a teacher. Nearly everyone has developed at least a few skills in this manner. This category of assets becomes especially important for the person who has not worked before or who has not worked for many years. Even if you have been regularly employed, do not overlook these volunteer skills.

- *Personal Characteristics*
  Your personal characteristics are extremely important to your future success as a teacher in any area. In this section you will want to note a few of the traits that play a significant role in your ability to work with children or adolescents. For example, consider the importance of these skills: ability to work well under pressure, good sense of humor, drive, attention to detail, excessive timidity or nervousness, outstanding leadership qualities, and aversion to public contact. Looking at both your useful and not so useful characteristics can help you see the whole picture objectively. List your personality traits as assets or liabilities according to your own perception of how they have worked for you in the past—but be prepared to reconsider your categorization in the light of a new situation. In this section more than any other, an objective, mature, candid self-assessment is the key.

- *Mental Capabilities*
  The mental capabilities we possess can help us or hurt us as teachers. A mental capability that may be considered an asset in one situation could be a liability in another. For example, if you are able to keep things very well organized, this is usually a plus in teaching; however, if you are very dependent on order and must have a clean, neat, predictable environment, teaching in a classroom for children with emotional problems or perhaps in a middle school art room may prove too chaotic. It is therefore important that you look at your mental capabilities in light of the teaching position you most want to seek.

- *Physical Capabilities*
  When considering your physical capabilities you must again think about the different types of teaching jobs in which you have interest. Having good manual dexterity may be more important in one area of teaching, such as family and consumer education, than in a mathematics classroom. You might also want to look at your overall energy level and your stamina, especially if you are considering teaching in an area that requires you to be on your feet constantly—such as choral music director.

- *Flexibility*
  How many changes are you willing to make in your lifestyle to accommodate the mythical perfect job? If you are willing to relocate to a different city or state, this will be a definite asset, as will your willingness to take

courses on your own time to increase your skills. As it is necessary in most states to return to school to renew teaching licenses, your flexibility here is most important.

You may use this list as a reference for filling out your own self-appraisal.

1. *Education and Degrees*
   College courses and degrees; technical schools; college courses after degree; certifications, and what states they are good in

2. *Other Educational Experiences*
   Peace corps, seminars, workshops (not necessarily for credit)

3. *Work Experience*
   Names of employers, job titles, skills required, peripheral skills, equipment operated, internships, and so forth

4. *Hobbies or Volunteer Work*
   Teaching many skills (aerobics, karate, and so forth), learning to organize, Brownie leader, working in groups such as the Dane County political action group

5. *Personal Characteristics*
   Traits that make you especially good with children or adolescents, such as outstanding leadership ability, sense of humor, versatility

6. *Mental Capabilities*
   Very well organized (important when trying to deal with large groups of children and keep a classroom running smoothly)

7. *Physical Capabilities*
   Manual dexterity, athletic ability, in excellent health and able to remain on your feet for hours, able to keep up with five-year-olds

8. *Flexibility*
   Willing to travel one to two hours for a job in another district, able to take additional course work in the summer, interested in learning more about gifted children

Chart Your Experience and Characteristics

Now, as you begin to put this all together and gather all the experience and talents you have acquired, let's also put this information into a chart, so that it is easy to find when you need it. Remember to keep this handy for further development or improvement of your resume and for help before an interview. There are two basic charts, one for your experiences and one for your characteristics (see Figure 2.3.) Each one can help you pinpoint the things you will want to emphasize in your resume and in your interviews.

TIP   Save your experience and characteristics charts with your resumes; they can be used to prepare for each job for which you apply and each interview you want to take.

FIGURE 2.3.   Chart Your Experience

1. Education and Degrees

School Name and Years Attended	Degree	Honors, Major Courses, Special Skills, Major Accomplishments

2. Other Educational Experiences

3. Work Experience—Schools

School Name, Address, Phone Number	Job Title	Description of Duties Performed

(continued)

FIGURE 2.3.   Continued

4. Work Experience—Other

Company Name, Address, Phone Number	Job Title	Description of Duties Performed

5. Charting Your Characteristics

Describe Personality Trait	How This Has Worked for You
Describe Mental Capabilities	
Describe Physical Capabilities	
Describe Flexibility	

6. Chart Your Experience

Hobbies or Volunteer Experiences

Role	Responsibility	Special Skills/ Learned Accomplishments

What Do I Have/What Do I Need?

Now, look over all the assets and liabilities you've written down in all of the diverse categories. Is there anything important about yourself, your background, or your characteristics that you've omitted? If so, jot it down somewhere, even if it doesn't seem to fit into any of the categories you've used.

In studying the facts you have recorded about yourself, you may well find that even if you have always held one type of job, the skills and characteristics you used there could apply equally well to a number of other jobs. This is where your own personal preference, as well as job availability, comes into play. For instance, if you are a math teacher who also happens to know how to weld, chances are good that you will wish to highlight your experiences and skills in the teaching field and play down your welding expertise. Nonetheless, you never know when someone will be looking for a teacher who can help out in the industrial arts room. If the skills you listed are many and varied, you may find it helpful to circle or underline those that you would most like to use or build on in your next position. Obviously, some people will have a wide range from which to pick and choose, while the scope of others may be fairly limited. Whether you have a myriad of teaching certificates or only one, you should be able to consider what area is most important to you and to determine in what type of classroom you could use these qualities to best advantage. This is the type of teaching position you should be seeing.

Granted, it's easy for us to say you should be selective. We are not the ones who are out of a job, and as one unemployed friend pointed out, you tend not to be so choosy when your children are starving! Nevertheless, you will never find the ideal job if you do not even know what its characteristics might be, and a great many prospective employees who have not analyzed their own assets do not recognize the ideal job when it is staring them in the face. Besides, experts tend to agree that it is unwise to tell a prospective principal that you will "do anything as long as you get a teaching position." However, they do want to hear that you are dedicated to children and are a caring person who will do whatever it takes to get the job. Often, filling a temporary position or accepting a teaching position for which you have no certification and no desire to teach can get you off to a bad start. Interviewers tend to be much more impressed by the motivation and maturity of applicants who have clear-cut ideas about the career paths they wish to follow, especially if their background and experience point in that direction. So, do start out by being selective. You can always become more flexible and relaxed in your criteria as your children grow hungrier.

TIPS   Be prepared and be sure the interviewer understands each point that you attempt to make.

When you leave an interview remind the interviewer that you are the best candidate and will support the district's and school's mission.

Not only do you want to inventory your basic skills and attributes, but you want to see if you can match your skills to those a school district needs. For example, you know that the Dotha Watose District has just received a grant to buy four new state-of-the-art computers for each classroom in their K–5 buildings. You have just completed a course on creative ways to use computers in the classroom. You could use this skill match to sell yourself; you could develop some interesting ways to use computers and discuss these in your interview; and you could add this to your portfolio. To help you discover these matches, try filling out the Teacher/School Needs Inventory (Figure 2.4), first with your skills and then for the needs of the different districts you want to interview with. These matches show you important ways to sell yourself.

FIGURE 2.4. Teacher/School Skill Needs Inventory

Place an X in front of the areas in which you have skill and/or experience. Place the district names in back of the areas you know the districts are looking for.

My Skills: **Districts That Need Skills:**

_____ **1.** Ability Grouping

_____ **2.** At-Risk Student Experience

_____ **3.** Attention Deficit Disorder

_____ **4.** Behavior Modification

_____ **5.** Bilingual

_____ **6.** Chapter Programs (list)

_____ **7.** Collaborative Group Work

_____ **8.** Computer-Based Teaching

_____ **9.** Cooperative Learning

_____ **10.** Direct Instruction

_____ **11.** Diverse Student Population Experience

_____ **12.** Drama/Dance

_____ **13.** Early Childhood (Preschool)

_____ **14.** English As a Second Language

_____ **15.** Experience with Students Having Exceptional Educational Needs

_____ **16.** IEP Development

_____ **17.** Integrated Curriculum

_____ **18.** Language Arts Strength

_____ **19.** Learning Styles

_____ **20.** Math Their Way/CGI Math

_____ **21.** Middle School Experience

_____ **22.** Multi-Aging Experience

_____ **23.** Multicultural Training and Experience

_____ **24.** Multidisciplinary Teaching

_____ **25.** M-Team Participation (Multidisciplinary)

_____ **26.** Outcome-Based Education (OBE)

_____ **27.** Peer Collaboration

_____ **28.** Peer Tutoring

_____ **29.** School/College Collaboration

_____ **30.** School/Community Collaboration

(continued)

FIGURE 2.4.   Continued

My Skills:	Districts That Need Skills:
_____ 31. Science Strength	_____
_____ 32. Signing Experience	_____
_____ 33. Strategic Learning Skills	_____
_____ 34. Talented and Gifted	_____
_____ 35. Team Teaching	_____
_____ 36. Tech Prep Programming	_____
_____ 37. Whole Language	_____
_____ 38. Writing/Reading across the Curriculum	_____
_____ 39. Learning Disabilities	_____
_____ 40. Mental Retardation	_____
_____ 41. Emotional Disorders	_____
_____ 42. Communication Disorders	_____
_____ 43. Hearing Impairment	_____
_____ 44. Visual Impairment	_____
_____ 45. Autism	_____
_____ 46. Traumatic Brain Injury	_____
_____ 47. Physical Disabilities	_____

After you have matched your skills with the district, school, or classroom needs, go back and make lists of what you and the job you are seeking have in common. Do this in preparation for each job in which you have interest before interviewing.

Checklist for Teachers

If you have approached the self-appraisal with absolute candor, digging fervently into both your background and your conscience for every scrap of information that could be pertinent, you now probably have a much better idea of (1) the sort of teaching job you find ideal and (2) what deviations from this ideal you would be able or willing to accept. You do not, of course, know exactly where this ideal job may be waiting, but that is not the point of the self-appraisal. Of much more importance is the fact that you are now prepared to create a resume that will stand you in good stead when the perfect opening does present itself. As a bonus, you have probably learned some things about yourself and your aspirations that will not go into the resume but will remind you of what to mention during the interview or to mull over afterward.

Now, what are some things you know you cannot compromise without doing damage to your ability to teach well? Some teachers know they cannot handle children who are extremely talented in the area of mathematics, as this is not an area in which they have training or aptitude. Some teachers may know that teaching band to middle school students, though related to their field of choral music, would be beyond their ability without further training. Make sure you are honest with yourself about what you can and cannot do or you will find your principal and yourself disappointed. It may be helpful to list on the checklist for teachers what you feel you can and cannot do, as well as what you really want in a position (see Figure 2.5, "Checklist for Teachers").

FIGURE 2.5. Checklist for Teachers

---

1. My ideal teaching job might be . . .

2. I'd be willing to accept . . .

3. I must have a position in a school/district with these characteristics . . .

TIP Be sure you are a good match for the job before you apply.

Packaging Your Military Experience for a Position in Education

Some candidates, both men and women, have had military experience, either in the full-time military forces or in the National Guard or reserve forces. Many of these experiences provided management skills and training duties that are readily transferable to teaching positions. Further, most people who have served in the military are proud of what they have done and may wish to talk about it.

So What's the Problem?

In today's world, fewer and fewer people have served in the military forces. Many people have formed their opinions of the military from viewing World War II or Vietnam War movies, from television, or from reading war novels that have given them biased opinions of military service. These factors should be taken seriously by anyone who is leaving the military service and seeking a position in the educational world.

Since the Vietnam era, the military forces have undergone dramatic changes. Congress abandoned the draft and went to an all-volunteer military structure. Madison Avenue marketing and advertising firms were employed to give the military a fresh image and attract better qualified people for the "techno" forces of the new military. Education and intelligence requirements became more stringent, and pay grades and promotional opportunities were made attractive so as to enable the military to compete in the labor market for higher quality recruits. There are more opportunities for women and minorities, and the whole culture of the old military is changing. Big-stick management and and strict military discipline are giving way to team building and an emphasis on leadership skills. Flexibility, together with a premium placed on interpersonal skills, is becoming the order of the day in the modern military forces.

How can recently separated military persons transfer their acquired skills to the world of education? Let's refer to some characteristics of successful educators.

1. *Adaptability:* Adaptability means being able to adjust teaching programs and classroom environments to meet the needs of a particular group of students.

   Most individuals with military background who have been involved in training activities can readily adjust to these situations.

2. *Ability to manage or organize:* Teachers must manage large groups of children, often with varying skills and abilities, through learning activities in many types of conditions and settings.

   The ability to manage or organize is an essential condition of high-level noncommissioned officers. Junior officers are required to attend supervisory and management schools in order to be promoted to command positions.

3. *Planning and Preparation:* Planning and preparation are very important parts of any teacher's job. Teachers are often required to turn in weekly lessons plans before the beginning of each week.

   Planning and preparation are also important parts of the military. Military people are taught to plan carefully, think ahead, and develop contingency plans in order to be prepared to handle any unusual situations that may come up. This is not unlike preparing preventive discipline plans for coping with classroom behavior problems.

4. *Interpersonal skills and situational awareness:* Interpersonal skills and situation awareness involve the ability to be cognizant of problem areas while being available to assist students who need help and mentoring.

   Both of these skills are extremely important in the military. Imagine the importance of situation awareness when you are responsible for ten to thirty-five students for seven hours a day five days a week. How many parents have difficulty keeping track of two or three children?

Empathy: Empathy is being sensitive to students and having the ability to relate to each student's uniqueness.

The military is also learning to adapt to the uniqueness of its personnel in order to develop a successful fighting force.

As you can see, these characteristics of successful teachers are shared by mature military people who have extensive supervision and training responsibilities, often under highly stressful conditions. You will find the general-purpose resume of Jonathan, an ex-military person, in the next chapter.

3 Your Resume, or Why I Can Teach

This chapter was developed to help you develop multiple resumes to suit your individual needs.

OUTLINE

Case Study

Part A.   The General-Purpose Resume

Part B.   The Job-Specific Resume

Part C.   The Skill-Specific Resume

Part D.   The Alternate Resume

COMPETENCIES COVERED IN CHAPTER 3

Part A.   The General-Purpose Resume

1. I want to develop a resume that is short, concise, and eye-opening, the purpose of which is to get my foot in the school district's door even if there is no one specific job I am applying for.

Part B.   The Job-Specific Resume

1. I have uncovered a job that I want to apply for, and want to develop a resume that highlights the specific qualifications that make me an excellent candidate for the position.

Part C. The Specific-Skill Resume

    1. I want to develop a resume that highlights my skills versus my aptitude for a certain job. (This skills resume would also be a good resume if you knew you had much experience and many of the skills desired for a particular district or school.)

Part D. The Alternate Resume

    1. I want to develop a resume that leaves out dates. (Note: This would be useful if you have been out of work for a while, and you wish to develop an alternate resume.)

CASE STUDY

Candice has been teaching for twenty years. She has been a well-loved part of the small community of Oshberg for the past eleven years. She has touched the lives of many individuals and loves her job. However, Ray Anne, her daughter, has health problems, and they were advised to move to Arizona, where the drier air might improve her health. Although she is not eager to give up her friends, her job, and the home in which she and her husband raised their children, together the family has decided that what is most important is Ray Anne's health. Although moving was not something she would have chosen for herself, Candice realizes that change can be a good thing and that the winters in Arizona will be much easier to handle as the years roll on. So, after all these years, she is again in search of a job. Her husband will be moving in three months, and she will stay in Oshberg to finish out the school year, which will also allow her son to complete his senior year of high school. She must quickly put together her resume, as it is now February and she needs to begin sending out her vita as soon as possible.

    Candice began by developing a cohesive self-appraisal analysis. From this she developed a general-purpose resume. As her job search continued, she developed both job-specific resumes and skill-specific resumes. We will discuss both and will show you as well the resume of a newly graduating student, Jason, and that of an individual leaving the military, Jonathan (see Box 3.1, 3.2, and 3.3). You will see that they each have a uniqueness and may serve different purposes. If you are trying to develop a resume, it will be much easier if you have first completed a self-appraisal analysis, as described in Chapter 2.

The General-Purpose Resume

Much has been written about the format of the perfect resume, but most employers are more interested in the content of your resume than in the actual format. Since a prospective employer may form a first impression of you on the basis of your resume, you will want it to be neatly typed and well organized, and you will want to be sure to include, in a conspicuous spot, such vital data as your name, address, and telephone number. Beyond these obvious constraints, the content is the key to an effective resume.

The first question to ask yourself, before preparing your resume, is: What do I want this resume to do? If you are in the initial phase of your job search and are not yet applying for any particular opening, you will want the resume to open doors and help you obtain interviews. If this is the case, a short, attention-getting resume is recommended. "Attention-getting," by the way, does not mean "bizarre" or "flamboyant." It does mean a concise summary of your background, experience, and qualifications. Often, prospective employees mistakenly believe that the longer they can make their resumes, the more qualified they will appear to be. In actuality, however, the lengthy, wordy, overly explicit resume becomes a wastebasket filler rather than a door opener. Administrators want to know what skills you have mastered that will help them fill a need at their school right now, not every job and volunteer experience you have had since you were sixteen years old.

For some applicants, the one-page resume contains everything that needs to be said. A person who has worked since high school graduation filling bottles on a factory assembly line, while also going to school, might be hard put to come up with more than one page of pertinent information, even if describing the job in minute detail and listing twenty hobbies as a bonus. But another person might have several pages of jobs, skills, and activities to enumerate. Consider the accountant who is now interested in teaching business education. First this person attended business school, received several honors, and was active in a variety of organizations. After graduation, this person joined a private firm, then subsequently worked as part of the accounting department of a well-known major corporation. In both of these positions the experiences were varied and might well be spelled out in detail. Suppose, further, that this person is a member of several professional societies and also belongs to a number of worthwhile civic groups, thereby having accumulated a variety of skills—as an officer, member of the board of directors, and organizer of fund-raising projects. It is easy to imagine that this person's resume, even if concisely written, could run to four or five typewritten pages.

Most applicants agonize over restricting their resumes to a page or two, as they fear important data will be omitted. Remember that the task of the General Purpose Resume is to get a foot in the door for an interview. Some of the important information you want to share can be placed in a portfolio of sample work prepared specifically for each job interview. For example, where the initial resume states that you have conducted several workshops in your district to help other teachers upgrade their skills, your portfolio could list the workshops, with a brief summary of the content of each, or you could include some of the handouts and participant evaluations if you want to give further proof of your ability to run a meaningful workshop. Once you have made your initial impression with the concise resume and have gained an interview, you can produce your portfolio saying, "If you would like more information, I would be happy to share these with you as well."

TIPS   Supporting details of your skills and expertise usually fit well in your portfolio and can be used to produce samples during the individual interview.

Be sure you identify all of the training and skills you have that relate to the position for which you are applying.

Suppose, then, that you have decided on a general, door-opening type of resume about a page in length that can serve as your introduction to any district having an opening that interests you. The next step is to decide what to include in—and, conversely, what to exclude from—this resume.

First, a word about the personal data that usually appear at the top of the resume. These should certainly include the name, address, and telephone number of the applicant. Age (or date of birth), marital status, number of children, height, weight, color of eyes and hair—even race, nationality, and religion—are inappropriate to include in your resume or vita. Students sometimes ask us about including a photograph. Most employment experts feel that enclosing a photo with the resume is unnecessary, as well as expensive, and some employers even consider it ostentatious, self-serving, and in plain bad taste. Omit the photo, and keep the employer in suspense until the interview. Concentrate instead on selling your other qualifications.

Now we come to the heart of the matter—the portion of the resume that outlines your qualifications and experience. This is the part that can say to the personnel director, "This individual has skills that could qualify him or her for a variety of positions within our district," or "This individual is well-qualified for our high school science position," or "This person does not seem to have any particular skills to recommend him or her." Obviously, you don't need a resume that makes the latter statement. But, given a choice, which of the first two do you want to convey?

As you will recall, we said that you should be selective, at least at the outset, applying for jobs that suit your ideal. It might follow, then, that your resume should shout from the rooftops that you are qualified for one position only. But, as long as you are going to the trouble to apply, there's no use putting all your eggs into one basket when several baskets are at hand. By all means highlight those skills that you hope to utilize in your new position and those accomplishments that best reflect your ability to apply those skills. At the same time, though, mention your other skills and experiences, even if they do not apply to your current career goals. In the general resume, designed primarily to get you some interviews, you want to appear to have a wide variety of qualifications, even though the ones you place the most stock in will naturally receive the most emphasis. At the least, the inclusion of peripheral skills and accomplishments will make you appear well-rounded and versatile; occasionally, the mention of something you consider unrelated can be just the thing that makes the district personnel director feel you are uniquely qualified for the job of your dreams. For example, one woman applying for the job of second grade teacher mentioned that she had experience using a new "hands-on" science program and was hired over other equally qualified applicants because the district was starting to use this programming the following year.

In constructing your resume, then, refer frequently to your self-analysis chart and be sure that you are including all the assets you want to mention, with special emphasis on those you believe will be most important to the school system and the subject and/or grade level you wish to teach. Organize the body of the resume in a meaningful fashion, so that the readers can find what they are looking for at a glance. Many resumes begin, after the personal data, by listing education and degrees (including what the degree is in) chronologically. Next comes work-related experience (often listed in reverse order chronologically, since many applicants feel their most recent job is their most important one and should receive top billing). Don't forget to list your student teaching if you are a new or relatively new teacher. Finally, categories such as military service, honors and publications, and hobbies or outside activities might be dealt with. But there is nothing sacred about this order. If you feel, like Janet, that your most noteworthy accomplishments have come about in service to the police department, or, like James, that volunteer work with runaway teens gave you the most experience, by all means list this first and deal with the less impressive categories later. The most important thing is to present the material within each category (education, work experience, etc.) in a well-organized, probably chronological manner.

In describing each job, educational experience, or activity on your resume, try to be as specific and factual as possible while also keeping brevity in mind. Try to highlight your own skills and accomplishments rather than presenting a dry list of vague job duties or a standard position description. It is often helpful to the reader if you use bullets and verbs at the beginning of each skill or accomplishment you list. Going back to James, the individual whose most noteworthy accomplishment was in the area of working with runaway teens, initially he described his volunteer work as "Chairman of Parents Reach Out." Without any explanations as to what his contributions were or what the organization did, the principal reading his resume might assume he organized fund-raising activities such as car washes to raise money to help some unknown worthy group. However, he reworked this section of his resume describing in more detail what he accomplished.

- Developed a network between volunteers aiding troubled youth and multiple social service agencies, both private and public, to improve home situations for teens who have runaway from home.

Needless to say, the second resume elicited more interest from school districts because it specified the scope and importance of the project and clearly indicated that he had skills related to working with at-risk adolescents.

Now, what about all those wonderful personality traits, mental attributes, and indications of flexibility that you've listed on your self-assessment worksheet? Obviously, you can't write on your resume that you are bright, lovable, and drawn to all children. But you can often convey exactly that impression through careful wording of your accomplishments. Instead of saying that you're eager to learn, state that you took certain specific education courses to improve your teaching skills. If you have a science background but you also want to mention your leadership abilities and your knack for working well with others, highlight any experiences you may have had as the leader of a department that included these abilities. If you were previously involved with the police department, like Janet, and are unselfish and highly eager to meet difficult challenges, highlight the fact that you have these excellent attributes that would be a tribute to any school system.

TIP   We suggest you use bullets and verbs to begin statements about your skills and accomplishments.

Occasionally, an applicant will have a trait, quality, or desire that must be mentioned but cannot be worked logically into the body of the resume. This type of information can sometimes be given at the end of the resume, under Miscellaneous Information. Here, for example, a woman with a sales background, eager to develop new marketing classes in the business education program, can state that this is the case under Miscellaneous Information.

As a rule of thumb, liabilities on your self-analysis sheet need not be dealt with on the resume at all. If you are easily frustrated when trying to use the computer (which we hope you are not) or unable to spell, there is no need to point it out here; it will, no doubt, surface once you have obtained the interview, if it is an important skill for the job, or it will turn out not to matter anyway. The exception may be an obvious liability that you can maneuver until it appears to be an asset. For instance, a small community high school was looking for a math/science teacher. Most of the applications without both a mathematics and science certification hit the wastebasket. But the woman who got the job, although only certified in mathematics, had typed on her resume: "Although circumstances prevented my finishing my science certification, I have taken all but six credits of the course work and expect to receive my certification next semester." This applicant admitted her liability, described her efforts to overcome it, and was hired because she had described her progress in completing the needed certification.

Although some of the more subjective traits—mental abilities, personality characteristics, physical assets—seem out of place in a resume, especially if they border on bragging, they sound perfectly appropriate, oddly enough, in a cover letter. This is especially true if the letter is sent in response to a specific job opening in which that trait would be highly prized. It is probably not acceptable to put on a resume "good-looking, neatly dressed, pleasant personality," but it would be considered entirely tasteful to write in a letter of application, "My past experience has indicated that my friendliness and my ability to put strangers at ease would be definite assets in your early childhood special education position in which I will be entering families' homes weekly."

TIP   Remember subjective traits go into the cover letter very well.

There are three other categories of information that are sometimes appended to the resume, and these deserve mention here. The first is a statement that is generally headed Type of Position Desired. In the general resume, which is only intended to open doors, you might want to eliminate such a statement. If you are vague, it will sound as if you have no career plans or objectives; if you are very specific, it could work against you by eliminating some possibilities you hadn't yet heard of. You can always indicate the type of position you desire in your cover letter (tailoring your description, of course, to fit the district or the specific job opening). Cover letters will be discussed in more detail in a later chapter.

The second category of often appended information consists of references, both professional and personal. In many cases when your resume is sent out by a placement service, such as one provided by your college, three or four letters of reference are included when you request that your materials be sent to a school or district. Many districts have a standard procedure wherein application forms, resumes, and letters of reference are required before the application will be considered. If this is not the case, it may be to your advantage to indicate, "References supplied on request," and then to eliminate adding or naming them in the general resume. If a possible employer does not initially require them, you can tailor the references to the job needs once you have learned more about it. If you send them out before you know exactly what job or organization you're applying for you may well fail to include the names that would be most influential in a specific case. You probably won't want to list your current employer as a reference if you are discreetly looking for a job while you are continuing to work at your present position.

Once in a while, there may be some very important and influential people who are willing to give an applicant glowing references; if this is true in your case, it could be to your advantage to list these people on your general resume or in fact include their references with your application. Otherwise, it is perfectly acceptable to say, "References furnished on request."

Incidentally, while we are on the subject of references, always ask people's permission before listing them as references. Given a choice, it is also preferable to list those who are best acquainted with you and your work rather than those who may be higher up in the district but have had minimal actual contact with you. Your best chances for an excellent recommendation lie with those who know you, like you, are intimately acquainted with your work, and are expecting to be contacted for a reference. If you are not sure what someone thinks of you, do not ask them for a letter of recommendation or give their name as a reference.

Forearmed with your self-appraisal and fortified by the foregoing advice, you should now be able to write a general-purpose resume that will put your own best foot forward and pique the employer's interest sufficiently to get you an interview. Box 3.1 shows a sample of Candice's resume that was designed to serve a general introductory function to districts as yet unspecified. But remember: This is just one example out of a multitude of acceptable variations. The best format and structure for you is the one that most effectively highlights your own unique assets and qualifications. Several drafts may be necessary before you hit upon the best presentation, but the effort is well worth it if it opens the door to the ideal job opportunity.

TIPS   Don't forget to ask before listing someone as a reference.

Be sure to include your e-mail address, if you have one.

It is never wise to ask someone who barely knows you for a recommendation, as they will find the composition very difficult and may send a very bland, uninteresting letter. A reference cannot recount excellent traits they do not know you possess.

Never ask someone for a reference if you have had any difficulties or misunderstandings with them. (Something that to you may seem minor, such as a disagreement about a grade, may have been highly disturbing to the individual you disagreed with. After such an episode, they may see you as demanding or as a troublemaker.)

As you are contemplating the resume that Candice has written, let us consider the other candidates applying for jobs at the same time. What could newly graduating students do to make their resumes look appealing even though they have not yet taught for pay in full-time teaching jobs?

One important thing they can do is highlight their student teaching and practicum experiences. And if they have received some payment for their student teaching in the form of an internship, all the better.

Let's see what kind of resume Jason has as a new teacher entering the workforce. He needs to emphasize the multiple experiences he has had before

BOX 3.1 The General-Purpose Resume

Candice M. Barke email # cbarke@AOL.com
812 B. Eagle Street H# (414) 233–7271
Oshberg, WI 54999 W# (414) 233–2611

Professional Objective
 Teaching position in a special education program in public education

Skills
 • Experienced and interested in all levels of special education and in learning disabilities,
 emotional disturbance, and cognitive disabilities.
 • Experienced in special education inclusion and pull-out programs
 • Skilled in Direct Instruction and Project Read
 • Experienced in training teachers in regular education/special education collaboration

Education
 MA. University of Wisconsin–Madison in special education, August 1978
 B.S. University of Maryland in elementary education, December 1975

Professional Certification
 State of Wisconsin Teacher Certification in the areas of
  5-year license, Mental Retardation K–12
  5-year license, Emotional Disturbance K–12
  5-year license, Learning Disabilities K–12
  5-year license, Elementary Education 1–8

Teaching Experience
 • Teaching Faculty, Oshberg High School, Oshberg, Wisconsin, Program for the
 Learning Disabled and Emotionally Disturbed,1985–1997
 • Teaching Faculty, Good Earth Grade School, Oshberg, Wisconsin, Program for the
 Mentally Retarded and Emotionally Disturbed, 1983–1985
 • Teaching Faculty, Sherman Meyer High School, Loyaland, Wisconsin, Program for
 the Emotionally Disturbed and Learning Disabled, 1977–1983
 • Teaching Assistant, University of Wisconsin-Madison, 1976–1977

Memberships
 Council for Exceptional Children:
  Division for Learning Disabilities; Council for Children with Behavioral Disorders

Other Activities
 President of the Wilson School Parent-Teacher Organization
 Core Group Member, Oshberg High School District AODA Committee

Credentials
 Educational Placement and Career Services
 B150 Education Bldg, 1000 Bascom Hall
 Madison, WI 54706

---

finishing his degree. Jason picked up a lot of good ideas in the many classrooms in which he was involved. He also learned a great deal about displaying art in schools and local businesses. How can he highlight this to his advantage? See Box 3.2.

Remember that in Chapter 2 there was a section on Packaging Your Military Experience for a Position in Education? We have included here the resume of Jonathan, who had experience in the military and is now looking for a teaching job. Notice how he describes his experience and highlights his skills working with culturally diverse populations and coordinating groups.

Looking at the resume that Jonathan developed, do you feel his experience is unique and valuable? Do you think a district will see value in his experience even though he has not taught at the middle school level before? What

---

BOX 3.2   The General-Purpose Resume for a Newly Graduating Student

---

Jason Broom   email # jbroom@AOL.com
842 Sparrow Street   H# (414) 238–7331
Oshberg, WI 54999   W# (414) 233–5411

Professional Objective
    Teaching position in a middle school or high school art program in public education

Skills
- Experienced at both 6–8 and 9–12 grade levels of art education
- Special interest in working with students with disabilities
- Background in arranging art shows
- Master potter
- Talented in creating constantly changing high-interest displays of art throughout school buildings

Education
    B.S. University of Wisconsin–Madison in art education, August 1998

Professional Certification
    State of Wisconsin Teacher Certification in the area of:
        5-year license, art education 6–8
        5-year license, art education 9–12

Teaching Experience
- Internship as faculty, Newberry High School art program, December–June 1998
- Substitute Teaching, Earton Grade School, Watona, Wisconsin, 1997–1998
- Practicum experience, Sherman Meyer High School, Loyaland, Wisconsin, 9–12 art program, January–June 1997
- Practicum experience, Beacon Hill Middle School, 6–8 art program, August–December 1996

Memberships
    National Council for Art Education

Awards
    Reardon Master Potters Award

Credentials
    Available on request

else could he, as a newly graduating student, do to make his resume look more appealing since he has not yet taught in a middle school or high school?

One important thing to add and highlight would be his student teaching and practicum experiences. Although his background of teaching adults in the military indicates more than would that of an individual with no teaching experience, his student teaching experience will help him prove he can teach

BOX 3.3   The General-Purpose Resume

Jonathan M. Knight   email jknight@AOL.com
1615 North Street   H# (404) 663–7212
Atlanta, Georgia 99456   W# (404) 663–2617

Professional Objective
    Teaching position where I could use my training and supervisory background
    Preferably a social studies position at the middle-school level

Skills
- Proficient in teaching, training, and mentoring of multicultural groups in an educational setting
- Experienced in using Madeline Hunter's Critical Elements of Instruction
- Experienced in counseling personal wellness
- Skilled in coordination of groups, crowd control, and emergency procedures

Education
    B.S. University of Georgia, Athens
    15 credits to go to complete M.S. in education

Professional Certification
    State of Georgia Teacher Certification in the area of
        5-year license, Broad Field Social Studies 6–12
    Certified Instructor—Army Command and Staff School

Teaching Experience
- Student Teaching, Monroe Naperville High School, Monroe, GA, Spring 98
- Teaching Faculty, Armed Forces Management School, Fort Benning, GA 1988–1994
- Teaching Faculty, Noncommissioned Officers Course, Fort Riley, KA 1994–1998
- Teaching Assistant, University of Georgia 1999–2000

Memberships
    Council of Teachers of Social Studies
    American Society of Training and Development, 4 years District Chair

Other Activities
    Big Brothers—10 years

Credentials
    Credentials available on request through

    Educational Placement and Career Services
    University of Wisconsin–Madison
    B150 Education Bldg, 1000 Bascom Hall
    Madison, WI 54706

children. If you know something in particular about the job you are seeking, especially in a job-specific resume, you may want to be sure you add specific information to the resume about your student teaching experience. For example, Jason might describe the unusual duties he was able to perform, such as assisting in developing the K–3 after-school program, publishing a weekly parent newsletter, and coordinating the colorful pride program for a students-of-various-ethnicities support group, while student teaching at Monroe Naperville High School.

The Job-Specific Resume

Once they have structured and circulated a resume, many job applicants tend to think of it as the official resume, for better or worse. They may see an ad for a job opening that sounds appealing although it matches only some of the skills mentioned in passing on the resume. Nonetheless, they send out the same old resume, moaning all the way to the post office about the fact that it doesn't quite do justice to their qualifications for this particular job.

This one-track mentality is, of course, unnecessary and self-defeating. Theoretically, a person can have any number of resumes all highlighting slightly different skills and strengths, each one as truthful as the next. If you hear of an opening for a specific job that intrigues you, take a long, analytical look at your general resume. To the best of your knowledge, what skills is the school likely to be looking for? What characteristics would the ideal teacher for this position possess? Do you have these skills and characteristics? And, more important, does your resume highlight the fact that you possess them? If the answer to the former question is yes but that to the latter no, revise the resume before you send it in! In other words, tailor it for this one opening, structure it to read (insofar as honesty allows) as if you were the answer to the principal's prayers. You might even go so far as to indicate your career goals, or Type of Position Desired, on this individualized version, while taking care to avoid duplicating the job description. If you do indicate your goals, be reasonable; keep in mind the fine line between candor and wishful thinking.

Boxes 3.4 and 3.5 are examples of Candice's job-specific resumes. In these examples, however, Candice is applying for two specific and rather different jobs.

1. Can you see what job she is applying for using the first job-specific resume in Box 3.4?
2. How about the second job opening in Box 3.5?
   Now look at the resume of our newly graduating teacher, Jason Broom (Box 3.2). He is most interested in a job at a middle or high school. He has included things he hopes will spark the schools' interest in him.
3. What about Jason Broom's vita? Do you think his resume will accomplish this task?

Boxes 3.4 and 3.5 are examples of Candice's job-specific resumes. (Box 3.1 is her general-purpose resume.) In Job-Specific Resume 3.4, Candice is applying for a high school position as a teacher of students with learning disabilities. As you can see, she clearly states this under her professional objective. She highlights her special education background and experiences, including testing and Individual Education Plan preparation. She also describes her lifetime license in learning disabilities K–12 first under Professional Certification, even

BOX 3.4   The Job-Specific Resume

Candice M. Barker   email# cbarker@compuserve.com
812 B. Eagle Street   H# (414) 233–7217
Oshberg, WI 53991   W# (414) 233–2611

Professional Objective
Teaching position in a high school program. Experienced and most interested in the area of Learning Disabilities.

Positions Held
- Teaching Faculty, Good Earth Grade School, Oshberg, Wisconsin, Program for the Mentally Retarded and Emotionally Disturbed, 1983–1990
- Teaching Faculty, Sherman Meyer High School, Loyaland, Wisconsin, Program for the Emotionally Disturbed and Learning Disabled, 1977–1983
- Oshberg High School, Oshberg, Wisconsin, Program for the Learning Disabled and Emotionally Disturbed,1983–1999
- Teaching Assistant, Exceptional Children and Youth, University of Wisconsin–Madison, 1976–1977

Teaching Experience
While teaching in the public schools during the past twenty years I have been very involved in
- special education integration
- student screening and multidisciplinary team evaluations
- curriculum development
- Individual Education Plan preparation
- facilitating large and small group discussions
- test preparation, administration, and scoring of at least twelve different standardized tests; development and administration of innumerable criterion-referenced tests; serving the needs of the students in regular education classrooms through team teaching and teacher consultation
- serving the exceptional education needs of the students in my programs

Professional Certification
State of Wisconsin Teacher Certification in the areas of:
        Life license, Learning Disabilities K–12
        Life license, Emotional Disturbance K–12
        5-year license, Mental Retardation K–12
        5-year license, Elementary Education 1–8

Education
MA. University of Wisconsin-Madison in special education, August 1978
B.S. University of Maryland in elementary education, December 1975

Candice M. Barker

Special Workshops/Conferences Attended
- WDPI Special Education Transition-to-Work Workshop
- Wisconsin Learning Disabilities Conference
- Behavior Disorders Workshop: Helping Students Reach Their Potential
- Serving Special Needs Students in the Regular Classroom
- Everyday Math Workshop
- Dealing with Diversity in the Classroom

Memberships

Council for Exceptional Children
  Division for Learning Disabilities
  Council for Children with Behavioral Disorders
Curriculum Development Association

Other Activities

President of the Wilson School Parent-Teacher Organization
Core Group Member, Oshberg High School District AODA Committee

Credentials

Credentials available on request through

Educational Placement and Career Services
University of Wisconsin–Madison
B150 Education Bldg, 1000 Bascom Hall
Madison, WI 54706

though her first license earned chronologically is in the area of elementary education. Please notice also that her professional memberships list special education organizations, such as a learning disabilities/behavioral disorders organization, first.

In Box 3.5 Candice has decided it might be interesting to try to reenter the field of regular education classroom teaching using her special training as a helpful addition to her regular, elementary school 1–8 certification. As you can see, her professional objectives reflect this change in focus as does her description of her teaching experience and the order in which she lists her teaching licensure, professional memberships, and special workshops

BOX 3.5   The Job-Specific Resume

Candice M. Barker   cbarker@compuserve.com
812 B. Eagle Street   H# (414) 233–7217
Oshberg, WI 53991   W# (414) 233–2611

Professional Objective
   Teaching position in an elementary school program. Experienced and most interested in working in a regular classroom integrated with special needs students. I would like to expand my career in the area of regular education classroom teaching as I feel I have the training and skills to individualize instruction and meet the needs of all my students in a regular classroom setting.

Positions Held
   • Teaching Faculty, Oshberg High School, Oshberg, Wisconsin, Program for the Learning Disabled and Emotionally Disturbed,1985–1997
   • Teaching Faculty, Good Earth Grade School, Oshberg, Wisconsin, Program for the Mentally Retarded and Emotionally Disturbed, 1983–1985
   • Teaching Faculty, Sherman Meyer High School, Loyaland, Wisconsin, Program for the Emotionally Disturbed and Learning Disabled, 1977–1983
   • Teaching Assistant, Exceptional Children and Youth, University of Wisconsin–Madison, 1976–1977

Teaching Experience
   • planned, developed, implemented, and evaluated special education curriculum
   • spearheaded an intense faculty inservice and student screening program for regular and special educators
   • facilitated and monitored group work using cooperative learning in various classroom settings
   • developed a model program for special education faculty to facilitate large-group instruction in regular education classrooms
   • served the needs of the regular and special education students in regular education classrooms through team teaching and teacher consultation
   • integrated and adapted special education curriculum into the regular education classroom

Professional Certification
   State of Wisconsin Teacher Certification in the areas of
         5-year license, Elementary Education 1–8
         5-year license, Mental Retardation K–12
         Life License, Learning Disabilities K–12

Education
   M.A. University of Wisconsin–Madison in special education, August 1978
         Life license, Emotional Disturbance K–12
   B.S. University of Maryland in elementary education, December 1975

---

attended. However, before Candice uses or even develops her resume to reflect an interest in a regular education position, we would hope she has given this a great deal of thought and is truly interested in returning to teaching in a regular education, grade-school classroom. Once she has done this, her resume can reflect her interests.

1. Do you think as a principal you would want to hire Candice?
2. Would you hire her for either position? Why or why not?

Candice M. Barker   page 2

Special Workshops/Conferences Attended
- Everyday Math Workshop
- Dealing with Diversity in the Classroom
- Serving Special Needs Students in the Regular Classroom
- WDPI Special Education Transition-to-Work Workshop
- Behavior Disorders Workshop: Helping Students Reach Their Potential

Memberships

Curriculum and Development Association
Council for Exceptional Children
      Division for Learning Disabilities
      Council for Children with Behavioral Disorders

Other Activities
- President of the Wilson School Parent Teacher Organization
- Core Group Member, Oshberg High School District AODA Committee

Credentials

Credentials available on request through

Educational Placement and Career Services
University of Wisconsin–Madison
B150 Education Bldg, 1000 Bascom Hall
Madison, WI 54706

The Skill-Specific Resume

Now let's look at Candice's skill-specific or targeted resume. Here she begins with a listing of her capabilities and achievements. As you can see, many of these achievements and capabilities are not easy to guess at in her first two resumes. Therefore, for some districts that may be looking for very specific capabilities, this might be the best way to highlight Candice's achievements. The capabilities in this resume are usually listed from beginning to end by most developed skill to least. However, if Candice knew the school district was looking for a specific skill, such as an individual who might volunteer to spearhead the AODA (alcohol and drug addiction prevention) campaign, then she might list that achievement closer to the top of the list to ensure that it is noticed. See the example in Box 3.6.

1. How would you, as a high school principal, feel about a resume like this skill-specific resume?
2. What if Candice really understood your district needs and was aware that your district was working toward full integration of their learning disabled students? Then, what skills would she like to highlight?

BOX 3.6   The Skill-Specific Resume

Candice M. Barker   cbarker@compuserve.com
812 B. Eagle Street   H# (414) 233–7217
Oshberg, WI 53991   W# (414) 233–2611

Professional Objective

Teaching position in an elementary school program. Experienced and most interested in working in a regular classroom integrated with special needs students. I would like to expand my career in the area of regular education classroom teaching as I feel I have the training and skills to individualize instruction and meet the needs of all my students in a regular classroom setting.

Positions Held

- Teaching Faculty, Oshberg High School, Oshberg, Wisconsin, Program for the Learning Disabled and Emotionally Disturbed,1985–1997
- Teaching Faculty, Good Earth Grade School, Oshberg, Wisconsin, Program for the Mentally Retarded and Emotionally Disturbed, 1983–1985
- Teaching Faculty, Sherman Meyer High School, Loyaland, Wisconsin, Program for the Emotionally Disturbed and Learning Disabled, 1977–1983
- Teaching Assistant, Exceptional Children and Youth, University of Wisconsin–Madison, 1976–1977

Teaching Experience

- planned, developed, implemented, and evaluated special education curriculum
- spearheaded an intense faculty inservice and student screening program for regular and special educators
- facilitated and monitored group work using cooperative learning in various classroom settings
- developed a model program for special education faculty to facilitate large-group instruction in regular education classrooms
- served the needs of the regular and special education students in regular education classrooms through team teaching and teacher consultation
- integrated and adapted special education curriculum into the regular education classroom

Professional Certification

State of Wisconsin Teacher Certification in the areas of
    5-year license, Elementary Education 1–8
    5-year license, Mental Retardation K–12
    Life License, Learning Disabilities K–12

Education

M.A. University of Wisconsin–Madison in special education, August 1978
    Life license, Emotional Disturbance K–12
B.S. University of Maryland in elementary education, December 1975

The Alternate Resume

If Candice has a large gap in her resume, due to being out of work or even raising a family, that she wants to play down, she can always use an alternate resume in which she leaves out dates or perhaps lists accomplishments without a job target. This resume is unique and may not be what the school district is accustomed to reading. It would be useful in specific situations, depending on the needs of the individual seeking a job. See example in Box 3.7.

BOX 3.7   The Alternate Resume

Candice M. Barker
812 B. Eagle Street, Oshberg, WI 53991
H# (414) 233–7217 W# (414) 233–2611
email#cbarker@compuserve.com

Job Target High School Learning Disabilities Teacher

Capabilities
- Experienced with both standardized test administration and interpretation, and curriculum-based assessment
- Administered, adapted, and developed assessment devices to use with challenged students in regular classes
- Prepared individual education programs for daily and monthly course of study
- Maintained order and discipline in large and small classes
- Counseled and directed children with learning difficulties to find positive solutions to problems posed by their disabilities
- Counseled parents and directed them to remedial action for specific learning, cognitive, and/or emotional problems of their students
- Trained and developed student abilities to transition into postsecondary programs or the world of work

Achievements
- Increased levels of reading at least 1½ grades in one year for all but one of twenty-three students on my LD caseload
- Developed new system for recording reading comprehension and reading recognition levels weekly, now used in all elementary special education programs with learning disabilities in the Oshberg District School
- Trained 15–17 learning-disabled children to achieve full integration in public school class within the first semester of school year
- Introduced real-life techniques for math learning into grade 2 with great success
- Founded district chemical-dependency prevention and intervention program

Work History
- Teacher of students with learning disabilities and emotional disorders, Oshberg High School, Oshberg, WI
- Teacher of students with emotional disorders and mental retardation, Good Earth Grade School, Oshberg, WI
- Teacher of students with learning disabilities and emotional disturbance, Sherman Meyer High School, Loyaland, WI

Education
University of Wisconsin–Madison, 1978—M.A. special education, 1975—B.S. elementary education

Certifications
Learning Disabilities K–12, life license
Emotional Disturbance K–12, life license
Elementary Education, 1–8, 5-year license
Mental Retardation 1–8, 5-year license

TIP	Any of these resume types may work for you in different situations, so try them all as needed.

The forms in Figures 3.1–3.4 are provided to make developing a resume easier for you. However, you may also find that your computer has options to help you develop your vita, so try that if you are able. The computer might be the easiest way to change and store your resume information.

FIGURE 3.1   The General-Purpose Resume

(name)   (e-mail)
(address)   (phone)

Professional Objective

Skills

Education

Professional Certification

Positions Held
(dates)

Memberships

Other Activities
(dates)

Credentials

FIGURE 3.2 **The Job-Specific Resume**

(name)   (e-mail)
(address)   (phone)

Professional Objective

Positions Held
(dates)

Teacher Certification

Professional Certification

Education

Professional Memberships

Special Workshops/Conferences Attended

Other Activities
(dates)

Credentials

FIGURE 3.3   The Skill-Specific Resume

(name)
(address)

(telephone)
(e-mail)

Job Target

Capabilities

Achievements

Work History
(dates)

Education History
(dates)

Certifications

FIGURE 3.4   The Alternate Resume

(name)
(address)

(telephone)
(e-mail)

Job Target

Capabilities

Achievements

Work History

Education

Certifications

CHAPTER

4 The Initial Contact: Where to Look

This chapter is designed to help you find out about job openings in your area of interest and/or certification.

OUTLINE

COMPETENCIES COVERED IN CHAPTER 4

Part A. Vacancy Listings

1. Will vacancy listings in the paper be of any use?
2. How about having my computer do the work?

Part B. Employment Agencies

    1. How might I use employment agencies both public and private?

Part C. College Placement Offices

    1. What should I know about college placement offices?

Part D. Conferences and Conventions

    1. What kind of chances do I have for finding a job at a conference, convention, or job fair?

Part E. Personal Contacts

    1. How can I get my friends involved in my search?

Part F. Blind Contacts

    1. What if I have no leads?

Part G. Asking for an Interview

    1. How do I ask for an interview by mail?
    2. How about by phone?
    3. Can I do it myself?
    4. How about having the agency contact future employers?

Part H. Job Search Organization

    1. How do I keep track of the position openings I am interested in?

CASE STUDY #1
"Go with the flow, the job will come to me!"

Diana had a very negative approach to the whole process of job hunting. In seeking part-time work while going to school she had had a number of poor interview experiences. Not unusual, when looking for temporary work. But all of this was a real turnoff and resulted in foot-dragging on her part.

She failed to use the facilities of her college placement office, which greatly restricted her outside contacts. She also missed the student teacher workshops on resume writing and interviewing. Despite the urging of her roommates, she skipped the job fair for teachers. When she went in for the screening interviews her friends had told her about, she came across to the interviewers as negative and defensive. (Unfortunately, the individuals interviewing her never called her back, so she had no idea why she was not called back.)

By late August, Diana was frustrated—she had no job and no leads.

1. How do you assess Diana's approach?
2. Would you change the approach she has taken?
3. If you answered yes to the above, how would you conduct your job search?

CASE STUDY #2
Control the Search

Jessica was a very organized person who approached difficult tasks with a plan and a timetable. She felt that source, contact, and preparation were the keys to a successful job search.

She started preparing herself in the fall term of her senior year by attending a resume-writing seminar. This was followed by a workshop in interviewing, which included simulated interviewing that was videotaped and critiqued. All of these experiences contributed to building her self-confidence and presence in the interview environment.

She took time off from work to attend the fall on-campus interviewing schedule, knowing that the spring interviewing would be too late. Furthering her experience, she attended two education job fairs to increase her contact exposure. The numerous interviews and job fairs resulted in six school-district interviews and three very good job offers. Her problem now was which one to pick—an enviable position to be in.

1. What is your opinion of the aforementioned approach?
2. Would you approach your job search differently? How will you approach your job search?

Maybe these approaches are too extreme, and you might choose to use a more "centrist" plan to enhance your opportunities in the position search. Whatever route you select, consider that the name of the game is contact, contact, contact. Maximum exposure to the job sources is essential to success.

Vacancy Listings

One of the most time-honored and still popular places to begin most job searches is in the want ads of the local newspaper. However, very few schools actually do their advertising in the newspaper. But for leads in some kinds of occupational categories, the help-wanted columns prove lucrative indeed. Generally, these ads cover unskilled, semiskilled, entry-level, sales, and clerical positions. As a rule of thumb, the more highly qualified or specialized applicants become, the less likely they will be to find the ideal job listed in the local want ads. Like most rules, however, this one has its exceptions. Although not worth spending much time on, it does not hurt to scan the local newspaper ads.

During the job-hunting period, people who live in small towns would be well advised to peruse not only the local want ads but also those in the newspapers of the nearest large city and of the state capital. This is especially true if you are willing to relocate to the larger city or capital. Surprisingly, you might find a job advertised there that is located close to your current home. It might also be helpful to look for ads in the newspapers of many large nearby cities. Most professional ads will be larger and more prominent than run-of-the-mill want ads. Usually the positions advertised in display ads are for professional, technical, and managerial persons, and these jobs may be local or farther afield.

Professional educators, especially if they are willing to relocate, may find that the trade and professional journals, such as *The Chronicle of Higher Education,* are their best sources of leads. Many of these have classified sections including help-wanted ads, especially for highly specialized and high-level administrative positions that would be difficult to fill through local recruiting. Administrators tend to advertise for help in the publications that they themselves read regularly.

In both the local media and the trade or professional press, one sometimes sees situation-wanted ads in addition to the more abundant help-wanted variety. These are ads purchased by the person who is looking for the job; they announce the job hunter's availability and qualifications. As a rule, advertising your availability in this manner is a waste of money, since prospective employers don't read the situation-wanted column.

Another easy way to start might be to check the journals of the largest teacher organization in your field. For example, a social studies teacher may find multiple listings in the Ohio Council for the Social Studies.

TIPS Finding a job in the want ads is a long shot, so if your time is limited try to spend your time more wisely by looking elsewhere.

Use the Internet for state departments of educations and school board information.

Web Sites

Fortunately there is a new way to search for teaching jobs that can be especially helpful for an individual who is willing to relocate. Now we have available to us electronic job hunting. This is not exactly the answer to everyone's prayers; however, it can be used along with conventional job search programs. If you are looking for a job in another part of the country this may be the best place to start.

Whether you are hooked up to Prodigy, America On Line, or Compu Serve, or have a web hookup through your library, school, or present job, there will be thousands of sites, any one of which could be the one to help you find a job in your field. The key is narrowing down the search. Three places in particular can be a great help to you.

- Career information services. Career information services can give you advice on interest areas, job availability, how to write your resume, and how to look for a job.
- Resource data banks. You can post your own resume in the resume bank and think how many people could see it.
- Job banks. Job banks have a listing of open positions across the country. This could be especially helpful if you are looking for a job in another geographical area.

Career Search on the World Wide Web. There are many helpful sites on the Internet. In fact many placement services at colleges and universities have excellent Web sites to help college students and alumni find jobs. For example, one especially good site was developed by the University of Wisconsin–Madison School of Education Educational Placement and Career Services, which can be reached at http://careers.soemadison.wisc.edu. This site has an on line workshop to help you use the World Wide Web in your job search. It includes information on all of these topics:

- About using the World Wide Web
- Strategies for using the Web
- Specific listings
- Learning about employers

Remember that when you are using the World Wide Web you are not only helping your job search but you are actually increasing your job qualifications by becoming Internet literate. Be sure to add the Internet and the World Wide Web to the list of special skills on your resume.

How to Get Started on the Web. In order to get started on the Web, if you are new at it, you may need to understand how the World Wide Web works. Here is how it is described by the University of Wisconsin–Madison Educational Placement and Career Services.

What is the World Wide Web? A system that lets you use a computer and browser software (like Netscape) to search for information all over the world. How do I get started using it?

1. Get to a computer with Internet capabilities and with a Web browser. Just ask, "Can I do the World Wide Web on this computer?" A lot can be done by just pointing and clicking with your mouse.

2. Read a book on using the Web. Libraries and bookstores are loaded with them.

3. Take a short course on the Web at a nearby computer store, technical college, or university.

4. Get a friend to help you. This may be the best choice of all.

5. Use a World Wide Web on-line tutorial.

Strategies I Could Use to Help My Job Search.   When using the Web for your career search, the first thing you should do is broaden your thinking about conducting a career search on the Web. Most people think only of getting vacancy listings on the web. In fact, employers and university career offices are just beginning to learn how to post positions on the Web. It is still true that most actual listings on the World Wide Web are for technology careers. While there are listings on the Web, many people overlook the unique power of the World Wide Web that allows people to get in contact with employers in ways that were not possible before. For example, teachers often want to learn more about school districts. Now they can go directly to the Web to find out about school districts. The same is true for other professions.

Specific Listings: Where Can I Find Actual Vacancy Postings?   You can search directly at university Web sites and at school district Web sites (see Information about Employers for more on this). Search engines such as Yahoo usually have employers listed by type. Also, there are many career-specific sites that can provide you with ideas for searching.

Sometimes you can do on-line searches, as you can with Project Connect. You may wish to do broad searches. For example, start by checking the whole state.

If the Web site doesn't have an on-line search, you can use the browser's find function. Use e-mail to contact them, if possible.

A Word of Warning: There are sometimes problems with Internet listings being dated. Vacancies usually have to be entered by people at the Web site. They can get behind. Probably the greatest opportunity on the Web is that of finding out about employers.

Learning about Employers.   This really only scratches the surface of possibilities for information about schools on the World Wide Web. Look for more additions to this list, and, of course, there are also the sources you will find on your own (University of Wisconsin–Madison School of Education Educational Placement and Career Services, 1998).

While you are checking your trade journals for information about jobs, you will also see statements such as this:

> For more information on the Boitis School District, check out our Web site at Boitis.k12.ca.us. (The certificated application can be found online.)

FIGURE 4.1. Career Information on the Internet

Some sites to check out	Addresses
1. Career Mosaic	http://www.careermosaic.com/
2. Career Paths	http://www.careerpath.com/
3. Cool Works	http://www.coolworks.com/showme/
4. Chronicle of Higher Education	http://chronicle.merit.edu/.ads/links.html
5. EDNET	http://pages.prodigy.com /CA/luca52A/bagley.html
6. Employment Resources for Language Teachers	http://www.tcom.ohiou.edu/OU Langauge/teachersjob.html
7. Employment Resources on the Internet	http://www.cs.purdue.edu/homes/swlodin/jobs.html
8. Job Search	http://www.lib.umich.edu/chdocs/employment/
9. Job Web	http://www.jobweb.org/
10. On-line Career Center	http://www.occ.comJocc/SearchAllJobs.html
11. Private School Job Listings	www.privateschooljobs.com/jobpage.html
12. Teach for America	www.teachforamerica.org/
13. The Wisconsin Employment Bureau	http://www.isgrp.com/web/
14. The Riley Guide	http://www.dbm.com/jobguide
15. YAHOO Education Index	www.yahoo.com/Education/K–12/

Be sure you check the Web site and, if at all applicable, fill out the application. What have you got to lose? Think of how quickly you can apply for jobs using this method. It is also an excellent way to learn more about the whole range of school districts' needs.

TIP   Many districts allow you to apply on line.

Employment Agencies

Another valuable source in your search for the perfect job is the employment agency. Agencies vary widely in degree of specialization, cost to the applicant, and potential effectiveness. Public employment agencies are those operated by the federal government, state governments, and some municipalities. Generally, state employment agencies are combined with unemployment compensation offices, so that the unemployed person who applies for benefits can also, at the same time, find help in seeking a new position. In our home state, these agencies are called Job Service Offices, and we believe this title is now used throughout the United States. This is a more appropriate name than the colloquial "unemployment" office, since many people mistakenly think one has to be receiving unemployment benefits before qualifying for job-hunting assistance from these offices. This is far from the truth, since any state citizen is eligible for the service.

Professional societies often run their own specialized personnel agencies for members. Educational organizations such as the state branch of the National Council for the Social Studies and the National Council for Teachers of English have personnel services for their members. These services are usually very helpful, since they deal exclusively with positions in your general field or area of interest. You can usually learn about these agencies at conventions of the society or through the society's publications. Be sure to check their Web sites, which are usually listed on any organization publications, or can be acquired over the telephone.

TIP Check your telephone directory yellow pages and find out what employment agencies your area has to offer.

Private Agencies

Few people in education are likely to go to private agencies and pay to get a job unless they are in very high-paying areas where they are badly needed and will be very highly paid. If this is the case, please read the next section.

Checklist for Use of Private Agencies

Agency Contacts:

1. Many private job service agencies are very professional, but some are not. Some may only help you with your resume and then give you lists with which to go out and hunt for yourself.
2. Be sure to find out up front who pays the fee. Some school districts that are hard up for a candidate might pay the fee, but most won't. Sometimes you can negotiate a salary that could include a hidden fee or expense.
3. Find out what contacts and job listings in your field they have before you agree to sign with the agency.
4. You will want to inquire into how many placements they have made and in what school districts.
5. Be familiar with their policies and procedures.
6. If you aren't satisfied initially or after a couple of weeks with any referrals, consider another agency.

7. It isn't a good idea to give any one agency exclusive rights to represent you to all possible employers. However, some will write this into your contract. Please read your contract carefully and discuss this if this is included.

8. If you have to pay a fee, be careful that it doesn't include add-ons—phone calls, faxes, computer use, and the like.

9. Many agencies have very high standards, but others don't. Follow the guidelines listed above.

10. You probably shouldn't consider a private agency unless you have exhausted all other available sources, as they can be expensive. (For example, they may charge a percentage of your first year's salary.)

There are exceptions to all rules. If you are a high-level administrator, principal, or superintendent with a salary in the high five or even six figures, it might be more advantageous to contact one of the numerous consulting firms or "head hunters" that specialize in these types of positions. They are privy to the listings of professional and high-level administrative positions nationwide. Most of them have detailed descriptions of the available positions and can provide you with negotiations assistance should you be a final job candidate. Again, be prepared to pay a high fee unless the hiring authority is prepared to pick up the fee. Often this is negotiable in high-level jobs.

College Placement Offices

There probably is no better place to begin your search than your own college placement office. Nearly every institution of higher learning has a placement office to serve its students and graduates. Many schools have offices just for the placement of individuals in education, and schools and districts of every size and variety recruit employees through these offices. Generally the director and staff of a college or university placement office are highly experienced professionals; their full-time duty is to assist students in finding jobs compatible with their education and to convince prospective employers that the graduates of this particular institution are better qualified than are other applicants. Although the college placement service is widely utilized by current students who are about to graduate, alumni often overlook it as a potential source of employment help. Yet these placement offices are also committed to helping with the placement of alumni, and they often receive requests for candidates who have experience as well as a degree. Since you are probably either presently a student or an alumnus of a college or university—even if you graduated longer ago than you care to remember—it could be well worth your while to contact both the alumni office and the placement office of your alma mater. You should furnish them with a resume and let them know what sort of opening you are seeking. Their services are either free to alumni or have a minimal fee, and once in a while they will even find a job for someone who is not a grad-uate, just as a favor to the prospective employer.

TIP   Your college placement office is probably the best single place to start on your job search.

Conferences, Conventions, and Job Fairs

A great way to meet many prospective employers at once is to attend a confer-ence or convention at which interviews are held as a peripheral activity. Job interviews are frequently found at a convention of an association or society for those employed in a particular discipline or specialty—science teachers, ele-mentary school teachers, special education teachers, and so forth. Here, recruiters from many districts may be available all day long, so those who attend the convention can stop by to see what jobs are available in the various districts and can perhaps have a screening interview on the spot (or make an appointment for one at a later date). An obvious advantage to this setup is that all the districts represented are interested in hiring people whose fields tie in with the subject of the convention or conference. Otherwise, they wouldn't bother to send a recruiter.

TIP   This is the perfect time to collect business cards and drop off your business card; be sure you take plenty along.

A bonus for the job hunter, or soon-to-be job hunter, at a convention is the opportunity to rub elbows with others in a given field or discipline who are gainfully employed and who may, in fact, be in a position to hire people. Con-tacts with them, on a quasi-social basis, may prove invaluable at a later date, even though these professionals may be from organizations that are not actively recruiting at this particular convention. Next year, when there is a job opening, it is always comforting to pick up the phone and say, "Remember me? We had dinner together at the Colorado Science Teachers Convention in Den-ver last summer." Less frequently, recruiters may attend job conferences or job fairs that concentrate on a certain segment of the population rather than a par-ticular field. For example, in recent years conferences for female administra-tors have grown in popularity. At these conferences, women are informed about how to get ahead in the world of school administration, how to counteract dis-crimination, and so on. Similar conferences are held for individuals from differ-ent ethnic backgrounds and other special groups who hope to find employment or upgrade their current positions. Although people attending such conferences usually pay a fee to do so, it may be worth your while simply to gain entry to the interviewing area if there are to be many districts represented.

In either case—convention or conference—do not expect to be hired on the spot. Just like college recruiters, the interviewers there are sent to screen for viable applicants, not to hire. If they are interested in you, they will notify the district and recommend that you be interviewed in more depth.

TIPS   Remember the individual sitting next to you today at the conference might be the person interviewing you next week or three years from now for your ideal job.

Check the bulletin boards for possible leads, while attending conferences.

Remember to go to every booth at a job fair because you never know what contact will help you in the future.

Personal Contacts

Personal acquaintances are among the best sources of leads for job openings. Even if you are utilizing several other sources in your search for the perfect job, be sure to let your friends, relatives, and former colleagues know you are looking. Make a special point of talking with acquaintances who are in the same general line of work as the field that interests you or who work for a district that you think you would like to join. Those who already work in a particular school or department are most likely to hear of related job openings first, before they have even been advertised. They may also know, even before the principal is aware of it, of a coworker's intention to resign. Ask such people to keep you posted on openings they may hear of, whether current or potential. It helps to be among the first to apply for a job. Your acquaintance may also be in a position to put a word in for you later. Even if this is not the case, however, you will be a step ahead of the competition because you learned about the opening first-hand. (A word of caution, though: Asking a friend to get you a job or implying in any way that you would like to have his or her job can be seen as threatening or potentially embarrassing by the friend, so avoid these approaches.) If you are fortunate enough to have friends or associates in districts in your area, you may indeed have a bonanza. In addition to providing you with job leads and references, acquaintances already in the district can be an invaluable source of information about the district as a whole, the characteristics of the principal or personnel director selecting the new employee, and the nature of the position being filled. Such knowledge would assist you in tailoring your resume to suit the job qualifications and in making the best possible impression during the interview. One word of warning about friends, relatives, and acquaintances: There are many things they can do for you, but it is invariably a mistake to rely on them to actually apply in your behalf or to present your case for you. Depending on the situation, they might mention your name to the individual who will do the hiring, alert him or her to the fact that your resume is on the way, and mention that they believe your application merits consideration. If they feel so inclined, they may praise you in glowing terms. But you cannot expect that the school district will take the initiative and get in touch with you just because an employee dropped your name. You must initiate the contact, express interest in the position, present your qualifications, and ask for an interview. It may be helpful to mention the name of the employee who informed you of the opening, but only with that employee's consent. Otherwise you may cause trouble for someone who has "leaked" information that should have been kept confidential. You should also be fairly certain that your informant is in good standing with the administration. (Otherwise, the endorsement could end up doing you more harm than good.)

TIPS   Word of mouth is probably one of the easiest and most comfortable ways to get a job. But don't just wait around for this to happen.

The expression "a good friend is worth their weight in gold" can be taken literally.

The Blind Contact

If all else fails, if all your leads go nowhere and your sources prove unresourceful, you may have to fall back on blind contacts. This is known in some circles as "knocking on doors," and it consists of walking into the offices of a school or school district, describing your qualifications, and attempting to convince someone to interview you. This is not normally the most efficient means of seeking employment, but sometimes it seems to be the only avenue left open. Needless to say, positions are seldom obtained through blind contacts. But you should never feel embarrassed to try this approach. Many have done so, and some have succeeded.

TIP   Do not try walking into a principal's office without an appointment. This could prove highly annoying. Instead, see if there is someone in charge of personnel who knows about present or future job openings.

Asking for an Interview

Let us point out, first of all, that the applicant at the first contact stage is not asking for a job, strictly speaking, but is asking for the chance to be considered for a job. This distinction is important. Whether you answer an employment ad by mail or by phone or whether you drop in unannounced at the administrative/personnel office of a large school district, you will, in effect, be asking for an interview. The same is true if an employment agency makes this contact for you. The counselor will be asking the potential employer to grant you an interview, not to give you a job. Many prospective employees make the mistake of trying to get the job at the time they make their initial contact by mail or phone. For instance they tend to answer ads with three-page letters extolling all their virtues and begging the employer to hire them. This approach has several disadvantages. First, a busy individual receiving numerous responses to an ad will be inundated with paper and will want to look through all the responses and resumes quickly so as to determine at a glance which respondents merit an interview. A long letter or bulky resume, at this stage, may well hit the wastebasket unread. Second, if you get the interview, the interviewer may lose interest if you have already said all there is to say about yourself in the letter. Third, long epistles early in the game tend to sound either self-serving or desperate. Finally, there is a lot to be said for withholding some information until you meet and size up the interviewer, thereby learning all you can and enabling yourself to tailor your responses to that individual and the requirements of the job.

At the other extreme, though, is the applicant who writes or phones for an interview without supplying any background information at all. This can be equally self-defeating, since there is nothing to pique the employer's interest or indicate that you may be the right candidate to fill the opening. In other words, unless the employer has reason to think that it would be worthwhile to interview you, he or she probably will not do so. The key here is to catch the interest of the employer and to make a strong case for yourself. Once you get your foot in the door at the interview, there will be plenty of opportunity to further dazzle the employer with your specific talents and accomplishments. If you are answering an ad, there will usually be specific instructions about how to apply. For example, if an ad says, "Call Mr. Johnson at 282–5820 between 10 A.M. and 2 P.M. Tuesday," do exactly that. Attempts to beat the rush by calling on Monday, or at 8 A.M., will likely catch Mr. Johnson at a busy time or before he is prepared, thus irritating him and demonstrating your own inability to follow simple instructions. By the same token, if the ad says, "write, enclosing resume," do not try to get in ahead of the competition by phoning, even if you know whom to phone. If the ad says to contact the guidance counselor, do not try to practice one-upmanship by contacting the principal. In short, follow to the letter any instructions you have been given.

TIP   Remember, you are just asking for an interview at this time, so don't get carried away. The last thing you want to do is bore the individual you want to hire you.

TIP   Be sure to use the appropriate titles, for example, Mr., Ms., or Dr. When in doubt, always promote to Dr.

By Mail

If a letter is requested, our advice is to keep it brief and sincere, striving to catch the employer's interest without resorting to gimmicks. It should be in proper business-letter format, neatly typed on high-quality twenty-pound white bond or your own personal letterhead, if you have one. Lined notebook or tablet paper is out; so is "pretty" stationery or notepaper that comes in bright or pastel shades, printed with little apples or books, or anything that is in any way unprofessional looking. Use full-size sheets of paper, as small sheets are more easily overlooked in a stack of mail; and never, never use the letterhead of the organization that currently employs you. The letter should be one page or less in length, so that the employer can scan the whole thing, including your signature, at a glance. It should include your return address, and it should begin by stating what job you are referring to and where you saw the ad (see Figure 4.2 Hints for Cover Letters and Figure 4.3 Example Cover Letter). This can save a lot of confusion and embarrassment in the event that a district has advertised in various publications for a variety of openings at the same time. The letter should also (1) refer the employer to your enclosed resume, (2) politely request an interview at the employer's convenience, and (3) give the telephone number at which you can be contacted during the day. (It is important to repeat address and telephone number in the letter, even if they appear on your resume, since these papers tend to get separated in the employer's office if the response to an ad is heavy.)

FIGURE 4.2.   Hints for Cover Letters

☐ Use high quality white bond paper, 8 x 10″ (Don't use pretty stationery or lined notebook paper)

☐ Personalize the cover letter

☐ Proofread for spelling errors, typos, and grammatical errors

☐ Be sure all names are spelled correctly

☐ Be sure your letter is well spaced on paper with 3/4–1″ margins

☐ Clarify your reason for writing

☐ Describe what the school/principal/district has to gain by hiring you

☐ Highlight your qualifications

☐ Capture the reader's interest

☐ Give the telephone number at which you can be contacted by day

☐ Keep it short, no more than one page

FIGURE 4.3.   Example Cover Letter

Use Good Quality Paper/Laser Printer
(Letter in center of page, side margins ¾–1")

Letter Format

Your Street/Box Address
City, State, Zip
Date

(3 blank spaces between your address and employer's address)

Name of Person
Title
Company Name
Street Address
City, State, Zip

(double space)

Dear <u>Name</u>:

Opening Paragraph
(text single spaced)

Begin your letter with a description of why you are writing; name the opening or positions for which you are applying. If appropriate, mention how you heard of the opening and/or the district.

(double space)

Middle Paragraphs

In these paragraphs you should describe why you are interested in working for the school and specify your reasons for seeking a job in this area of education. Refer to your education and other relevant experience; be sure to point out your particular achievements and qualifications in the field. This should be your main selling area. Refer the reader to the attached/enclosed resume, application form, or whatever documentation you are using to illustrate your training, interests, and experience.

(double space)

(continued)

Closing Paragraph

Pave the way for an interview by asking for an appointment, and by giving your telephone number, and other information about how you can best be reached. Be upbeat.

(double space)

Sincerely,

(3–4 spaces)

Your signature
Your name typed
Enclosure

Beyond these basic elements, the contents of the initial letter will vary depending on the amount of information you have about the job and the company. If you are answering a blind ad with no details at all except that the school is seeking, say, grade six to eight math teachers, then there is not much use padding your letter with extraneous facts. Just include the aforementioned basics, enclose your all-purpose resume showing that you are an experienced and competent math teacher, and leave well enough alone. On the other hand, if you know something about the nature of the job or about the school, you may want to include a sentence or two (but not much more than that) outlining why you are especially well qualified for this particular position. You may also want to mention an unusual fact or two that didn't lend itself to inclusion in your resume (e.g., your ability to relocate to the West Coast if that's where the job is). But no matter what you choose to include here, be brief and end by requesting an interview, not a job.

By Phone

Many applicants are shy about phoning to request a job interview, but you shouldn't hesitate to do so if this is what you have been asked to do. In fact, phoning often gives you an advantage over writing in that you can usually obtain some information about the job opening and a little feedback as the conversation progresses. Just collect your thoughts before you call so you will not sound frightened or flustered; state your name and tell the employer that you are calling in response to the ad in such-and-such for a such-and-such teacher. Hesitate at this point before gushing on about your credentials. Chances are good that the employer will use the first pause to fill you in a little on the nature of the job before asking about your qualifications. Remember, any information you can get will improve your chances of saying the right things (and, perhaps, more important, prevent you from saying the wrong ones). If your pause elicits no information, just briefly tell the employer your qualifications. For example, "I have five years of experience in a 6–8 middle school mathematics teaching position with the Appleville School District." Then add something like, "If this would qualify me for the position you have in mind, I would like to come in and talk to you at greater length about the job." If, as the result of a phone contact, you are granted an interview, and if time permits, I would be inclined to follow up the phone call by mail. Of course, this is impractical if the

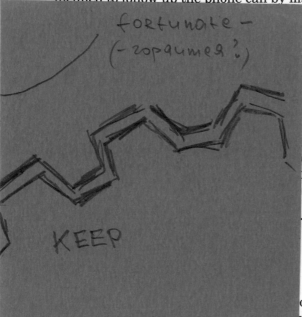

f it is scheduled a week or so ahead, it
irming the time of the appointment,
an interview, saying you look forward
esume that can be reviewed ahead of
s but also keeps you in the employer's
rgotten in the crush of calls from other

oducing yourself and then immediately
people know you are thinking of their
nity to speak to you when they are free

oach, your initial contact will have to
won't be responding to any ad or job
listing. Based on your extensive research of the district you intend to contact, you will have to determine whom to approach, how to do it, and what tactics to use. If you have pinpointed a specific problem you want to solve, or a specific contribution you think you can make, you may want to write to the principal at the school, outlining specific ideas that you believe could help the school, or a department, and asking for an appointment to discuss these possibilities. The very uniqueness of this approach may get you an appointment, since most principals are swamped with problems and it is very seldom that a stranger writes to volunteer help. This kind of letter is even easier if you can manage to meet the individual beforehand in a neutral setting such as a workshop, convention, or education course. Then, if your contact remembers you when you write for an appointment, you are much less likely to be turned down.

TIP It is not good practice to show up without an appointment.

The Agency Contact

Your responsibility for making the initial contact will be minimized if you are working through a placement service, an employment agency, or one of the government-run job service offices. These organizations will usually set up interviews for you and forward your resume to the prospective employer. Sometimes, however, the agency neglects to forward resumes or inefficient mail service prevents their timely delivery. If time permits, it is always a good idea for the applicant to send a resume directly, with a cover letter confirming the appointment set up by the agency. If time is too short, be sure to carry an extra resume to the interview in case the agency failed to send one.

Job Search Organization

A very important part of looking for a job is keeping track of the tasks you have completed and those you have not. This is especially important when looking for a job in education because teachers must be very well organized to be effective. Imagine if you were always losing things and you continually lost your students' work or their grades or you could not remember what you needed to teach your students and what you had already covered. You would probably be a rather ineffective teacher, and no principal wants a teacher who cannot keep the classroom organized. Therefore, it is especially important that, as an individual trying to impress the schools with your abilities, you be well organized and efficient in your job search. We suggest that you have a tracking system that you keep with you at all times, and one copy near the phone. You would not want to forget to send your resume to someone who is perhaps interested. And think of the confusion if you do not recognize the name of someone calling you back after an interview.

This organizer could look something like the one we have included here (Figure 4.4) or it could be one you have developed to fit your own personal needs. Regardless of what you use, make multiple copies of it and update it daily. This could save you from an embarrassing mistake that could cost you your perfect job.

TIP   Keep an up-to-date copy of your job-search organizer by each of your phones.

FIGURE 4.4. Job Search Organizer

MOFFATT & MOFFATT Job Search Organizer	Teaching areas	Grade level	Cover letter	Transcript Official or not	Send resume #1 or #2	Placement office credentials sent	Call schools? District reply?	Prepare for interviews	Initial screening interview	Teacher principal interview	Board interview	Follow up
Contact: School Address												
Contact: School Address												
Contact: School Address												
Contact: School Address												
Contact: School Address												
Contact School Address												

5 Presenting Yourself, or I'm the Answer to Your Prayers

This chapter explores the area of how to present yourself to possible employers in the best and yet most honest light. In the long run this will get you the job in which you will be most effective and content.

OUTLINE

COMPETENCIES COVERED IN CHAPTER 5

Part A. Understanding the School District's Needs
1. Can I stretch the truth to get the job?

Part B. What the School Distinct Is Looking For in a Candidate
1. How can I learn about what principals and school districts are looking for in a candidate?

Part C. Knowing the School District
1. How do I find out about a school?
2. Whom do I contact to get information about the school?

Part D. Looking and Acting Like a Professional Educator
1. What's the best way to dress?
2. What should I be sure not to do so that I won't turn off the interviewer?

Part E. Developing a Useful Portfolio
1. How can I use the portfolio?
2. How should I set up a portfolio to present to an interviewer?
3. What should I put in my portfolio?
4. How can I best use my portfolio?

CASE STUDY

Suzanne and Jennifer are both interested in the third grade opening at Middleberg Elementary School. Both women are newly certified and have not yet held a full-time teaching position. Their qualifications are quite similar and they are competing with each other as the top applicants for the position. It is Wednesday and both applicants will be interviewed next Monday morning.

Suzanne is outgoing and friendly. She exudes a certain affability and feels that her winning personality, along with her credentials, will carry her through an interview with flying colors. People seem to be drawn to her sunny disposition. She awaits her interview with confidence.

Jennifer is also well credentialed and eager for her first teaching job. She too is very friendly but perhaps a bit more serious and less exuberant than Suzanne. When she is called about her upcoming interview, she immediately plans to learn more about the elementary school and the Middleberg Hollow Unified School District. First she calls her neighbor, who has a son who teaches at the elementary school, and arranges to talk to him. She also stops by the Middleberg Hollow district office on her way home from work to pick up information about the school district, such as the administration, educational policy, budget, and hiring practices. On Thursday she plans to drop by the school in person to check that the secretary has her proper credentials and to thank the principal, through the secretary, for the interview. (She knows it is ill advised to drop in on a principal; they are very busy and may feel that an applicant dropping by is intruding and pushy.)

Fortunately, upon arriving in the office, Jennifer saw the principal who was just walking out. She never spoke to him, as she did not want to delay him, but she feels it will be easier to interview with him next week now that she has seen him and is more familiar with the school. She is also hopeful that the information she is gathering will give her a feel for the district and what she has to offer the school, and vice versa.

Although every candidate has their own style, it is very possible that the extra time and energy Jennifer put into preparing for Wednesday's interview will pay off, all things being equal. Even if the principal finds himself very impressed with Suzanne, he will probably remember Jennifer's note and might want to keep her in mind for the position.

---

1. Does your style best fit Suzanne or Jennifer?
2. If your style best fits Suzanne, what can you do to be more of a Jennifer?

Just like Suzanne and Jennifer, you will get an interview with someone who has a real, live job ready to be filled by some lucky applicant—maybe you! Although this is a major victory, the battle has not yet been won. Unfortunately for you, it's a sure bet that this potential teaching job will have others interviewing for it as well, so your job now is to present yourself during the interview so that you come across to your best advantage. Note, however, that this does not mean being deceptive about yourself in order to secure the position. Dishonesty, or even stretching the truth during an interview, can have all sorts of unpleasant repercussions and is never worth it in the long run. The experienced and perceptive interviewer will often notice your discomfort or pick up a flag that things do not quite add up and eliminate you from consideration. Even if you succeed in being deceptive and land the job that way, you will find that your prevarication has gotten you into a position you are unqualified for, unsuited to, or unlikely to be happy with.

Without being dishonest, though, there are several techniques that once mastered will help you present yourself—your *true* self—in the most favorable light possible, and we will discuss some of them here.

TIP   Just as working hard and doing your homework will pay off with good grades, working hard and studying the district's needs can pay off and get you the job!

Understanding the School District's Needs

All too often, candidates for a teaching job approach the interview by thinking long and hard about their own needs—type of school desired, salary requirements, and so forth—but failing to spare a passing thought for the school district's needs. Yet in almost every case, the applicant who knows the most about the needs of the school district, like Jennifer in the case described, is the one who will get the job, assuming his or her qualifications are equal to or nearly as good as those of other applicants. It pays to remember that your problems or fate as an applicant are not the primary concern of the interviewer. If a new employee is to be hired to perform a particular job in the school district, the interviewer's primary concern in the interview is to fill a certain position, and fill it in such a way that the performance of the new employee will reflect well on the interviewer and the school. During the interview, then, while the interviewer may express passing interest in your futile job hunt or your new baby or your virtuosity as a tuba player, he or she is really interested in learning only one thing: how well you can fill the teaching position that must be filled, and if hired, what kind of contribution you will make to the overall performance of the school, department, or grade level for which the interviewer has responsibility.

From the moment you meet the interviewer, there are things you can do to help him or her decide whether you meet the needs of the job. The first impression is critical. You must get the attention of the interviewer and do so in a positive way. The interviewer will be looking for a pleasant personality and for proper dress and grooming; we'll talk more about these details later in this chapter. But, perhaps more important, the interviewer will need to find out whether you are suited to and qualified for the job. Here you can be very helpful by having several copies of a well-prepared resume (even if you have already sent one by mail or given it to the employment officer) and a portfolio containing additional information and/or samples of your work. If an interviewer needs information about you that is not immediately available, he or she will be frustrated in attempting to assess your suitability for the job. As a result, you may well be omitted from consideration in favor of another applicant who does not present this obstacle.

As we said earlier, it pays to learn all you can about the department, school, school district, and community in which you may teach—before you appear for the interview. In the preceding chapter, we talked about the importance of knowing all you can about the school before you even ask for an interview and about finding possible sources of information in this regard. This kind of research becomes even more imperative when you are preparing to talk with the person who will ultimately choose the individual to be hired. Even if your interviewer does not expect you to know anything at all about the school, you will still be miles ahead of the opposition if you have briefed yourself. The more you know about the school and the community, the better you will be able to formulate your comments and responses to show that you would be able to meet the district's needs.

Although every employer's primary need is to fill the job, some employers are willing and able to wait longer than others to do so. In general, the smaller district's most critical need is to get someone on the job who can shoulder the workload right away; the school just doesn't have the resources to compete with the salaries of larger districts. If the need to fill the vacancy is immediate, you can use to advantage your ability to step right into the open slot. And if you don't have all the necessary certification, and are truly interested in working in a field with a shortage of teachers, you can help meet the employer's needs by offering to acquire necessary certification as quickly as possible.

If you are interviewing with a smaller district and you have done your research, you may also be able to sell yourself on the basis of your ability to teach in multiple areas. As we mentioned earlier, small districts often need someone with the professional versatility to perform in two or three related specialty areas. For instance, suppose the district has advertised that a school needs a fifth grade teacher. You also, however, happen to learn that the school has a large group of fifth graders and will need a middle school teacher next year, as this group of children move to middle school. You can demonstrate during the interview that you can meet their primary requirements as a fifth grade teacher and can also help them out in the future by being available to move up with the large class. This could be a very impressive bonus for the principal, who will have staffing problems in the future. In this case, the hours you spent researching the school's needs may land you the job, even though another candidate may be better qualified as a fifth grade teacher. Large districts, on the other hand, are more apt to be on the lookout for highly specialized teachers, for example, who can teach gifted children math and chemistry. Perhaps you have never taught gifted children, but you know a good program for modifying material to meet the needs of gifted children. You can tailor your comments during the interview to highlight your eagerness to gain additional training and to work with gifted children, as well as your ability to learn quickly.

Whether the district is large or small, the importance of selling yourself on the basis of the district's needs is especially significant if you are trying to change careers or if you are entering the job market after a long absence. You will have to be prepared to put your abilities on the line to show how they mesh with district and individual school needs. Furthermore, you will need to convince the interviewer that you are really committed to this new career. Your statements should be positive, though not unrealistic, and as specific as possible. Stress the personal sacrifice you have made (and are willing to make) to acquire new skills, your interest in and dedication to teaching, and of course the skills you can offer the school that will fulfill their immediate needs.

Perhaps the principal doesn't really know much about your field. A candidate who is knowledgeable about the school, the district and its little peculiarities and problems, and about the field in general can assist the interviewer by helping to determine existing needs. If you find yourself in the role of helping the interviewer do this, you will want to handle the situation in a very unassuming way. Otherwise, the interviewer will label you a know-it-all and consider you too presumptuous. This can be a very narrow line to tread. But if you use the right approach, you will have assisted the principal or superintendent simply by helping to clarify the school's needs, and you will find that your chances of getting the job have soared dramatically.

The art of pointing out to the district the nature of existing needs becomes all-important if you are pursuing the do-it-yourself approach. In this case, you are usually trying to create a job for yourself rather than fill an existing opening. It stands to reason, then, that your first and greatest task will be to convince the district that a need exists for a particular type of service and then to prove that you are the person who can alleviate that need more successfully and economically. Obviously, then, everything we have said about the importance of knowing the school district inside out applies doubly for the do-it-yourselfer.

Another way to help meet the needs of the school district is to answer questions cooperatively, candidly, and honestly. A straightforward and sincere approach on your part will enable the interviewer to determine the degree to which you will satisfy the job requirements. More important, in some instances your cooperativeness may help to put an uncomfortable interviewer at ease. You may fail to notice, because you yourself are apprehensive and anxious to make a good impression during the interview, that the interviewer is equally nervous. Yet this is often the case, especially among the inexperienced. Anything you can do to help put the interviewer at ease or to show that you have no ulterior motives will be helpful and, in the long run, increase the odds that your application will be favorably considered.

Such candor and honesty are not at odds with our earlier advice to highlight your strengths and downplay your weaknesses. It's a matter of emphasis, not of prevarication or avoidance. The trick is to sell your pluses in relation to the job confidently, without being cocky or egotistical, and to avoid mentioning your minuses unless directly asked. If you are asked a direct question that will force you to admit a shortcoming, try to answer it briefly but honestly and then explain how you hope to overcome this obstacle (e.g., through training, by substituting a technique with which you are more familiar, and so forth). Deal with apparent disabilities candidly. For instance, if you were recently nonrenewed at your previous district, explain the nature of the nonrenewal, stating how it is that you believe it is their good fortune that you are now available to fill a position in their school. Also indicate that you were ready to move on to new challenges.

TIPS   Don't forget that interviewers may also be nervous; you may need to help them relax.

Maintain eye contact without being too obvious.

What the School System Is Looking For in a Candidate

In the last few pages, we have given the impression that most interviewers will have a fair idea of the specific needs of the job, or the job *specifications*. Perhaps we should pause here to give the reader some idea of the way in which job specifications come into being and what they are likely to entail.

Once upon a time, principals did all of the interviewing of potential employees. Unfortunately, some principals were not very well trained in interviewing techniques. To be honest, they were often not trained at all. Of course, there were a few larger districts that had personnel whose sole job was to interview and screen candidates, and they had refined the selection process into a fine art. But when it came to the average school districts, some principals just didn't know how to conduct an interview or how to evaluate the various applicants and decide which should be selected for the job. Most of them recognized these shortcomings and felt distinctly ill at ease when thrown into the role of interviewer. As a result, these individuals often asked the wrong questions, got the wrong answers, and chose to hire those applicants they happened to like best, versus the applicants who may have been best for the job.

This situation is changing, especially in the larger school districts. Forward-thinking districts are starting to realize that the quality of their schools depends on the hiring decisions that are made and that many of these decisions are made by principals or administrators who don't know enough about the interviewing process. Districts are beginning to invest in professional training for those who interview by sending them to seminars on college campuses where interviewing techniques are taught. As these courses and seminars become more widespread, increasing numbers of individuals are receiving this sort of training.

One important result of this, for principals and district personnel directors, is that they are learning to assess the needs of the particular job that is open and then to evaluate the applicant in light of those job needs. From the district's point of view, this is a great improvement over the old tendencies to select the most personable candidate, the one with the most certificates, or the one with the most glowing letters of recommendation. There is no such thing as a "best" candidate across the board; candidates can only be evaluated and ranked *in relation to the job*. And these requirements, needless to say, vary from classroom to classroom and school to school. Good school interviewers will evaluate the needs of the school before they even start interviewing, and they will then conduct the interview so that it meets the ultimate objective of selecting the applicant who best meets these job-specific requirements.

One way in which the needs of the job are delineated is through job profiles. These are simply lists of skills and personal characteristics that have proved to be essential, or at least highly desirable, in the performance of the job in question. Profiles can be formulated at several levels, ranging from very general to very specific. (You will see a sample job profile in the case study in Chapter 6.)

A very general job profile might be assessed using an evaluation procedure that evaluates an individual's verbal answers compared to the answers of other teachers. After a school or school district has checked an applicant's teaching credentials and eliminated any individuals who do not possess the proper teaching licenses and credentials, they can require all applicants to take a test or participate in a structured interview so as to have more criteria to look at to systematically evaluate candidates. The test/interview can be given over the phone or in person. These interviews usually can be completed in an hour or less. They are frequently audiotaped. An individual who does poorly on a screener of this type may find it very difficult to get a job in any district that uses these devices. The kinds of questions you might be asked in one of these interviews are:

Why do you want to teach?

Do you feel you have something special to offer students and society?

Where do you get your greatest satisfaction in the classroom?

When did you decide you were interested in teaching?

What was the last conference or workshop you attended?

How are you planning on adapting to the individualized needs, interests, and abilities of your students?

Specific job profiles or teacher traits depend on the area in which a teacher may teach, as well as the grade level and configuration of the classroom and school. Imagine, if you will, the different requirements an interviewer would be looking for in a kindergarten teacher versus a high school biology teacher. Then think of the type of people you have known in these two very different areas. Consider two third grade teachers. One is teaching in a very traditional classroom in a religious school and the other is teaching in a newly integrated inner-city school that is multigraded and team taught with a regular education teacher and a special education teacher. The personality traits and teaching styles of these teachers need to be quite different. Although we like to think that a good teacher is a good teacher anywhere, I think you can imagine that certain individuals, while excellent in the correct situation, may be very unhappy professionally if they are placed in the wrong teaching environment.

This does not mean that a high school English teacher could never be a good grade school reading specialist. Changing areas of specialization and facing new challenges keeps teachers interesting and fresh. But getting a feel for the classroom and the types of demands a classroom or school will place on you will help you find your niche. Volunteering, team teaching, and visiting multiple classrooms will help you find a place where you can feel most valuable and comfortable. Knowing this about yourself will make you better able to "sell" yourself to someone else.

In many of the larger and more sophisticated districts, identification and relative weighting of these traits has become almost a science. When a particular job opening occurs, the interviewer will probably add specific requirements unique to this position. These job-specific requirements may take into account such variables as ability to work in crowded classroom conditions, behavior modification experience, specialized types of knowledge or experience required, and even the ability to deal with the personality quirks of key people with whom the candidate will have to cooperate. The best-trained interviewers know how to modify the basic job profile so that it clearly reflects the specifications of the job in question and how to evaluate each applicant in this context.

As you can see, the more you know about your own special field, the district, the department, and the interviewer, the better able you will be to figure out, prior to the interview, what skills and personal characteristics the interviewer will be seeking. If you have guessed correctly, you will be much better able—again, *within the bounds of honesty*—to present yourself as a person who possesses these skills and characteristics. By the same token, if you happen to be faced with an untrained interviewer who has not done his or her homework and does not seem to have clearly defined job specifications in mind, you will have an added advantage. You will be able, with the utmost tact, to help define needs for the *interviewer*—the highly professional interviewer as well as the completely inexperienced one. After all, interviewers are human beings. They have their own personality quirks and ideas, and they may evaluate applicants according to their own personal opinions and standards. Despite all they have been taught, some toss aside their job profiles and hire according to their gut feelings about the candidate. Others have so many biases and prejudices that they are simply unable to evaluate objectively a candidate who is, for instance, female, or redheaded, or overweight, or who previously worked in business.

Other interviewers tend to look for traits in the candidate that really have very little bearing on ultimate ability to perform the job. One example of this is the propensity of some interviewers to place a great deal of weight on the applicant's prior knowledge of the particular teaching material utilized by the school. Although these things could easily be learned by a new teacher, some interviewers persist in hiring the applicant who happens to possess these peripheral bits of knowledge even though the applicant ranks significantly lower on the traits and skills that are absolutely essential to job performance.

Finally, there are some otherwise adept interviewers who attempt to uncover desirable traits through the use of undesirable techniques. They may, for instance, try to put the applicant under a great deal of stress during the interview in order to see how the applicant will react to stress on the job. The problem here is that the two situations and the types of stress engendered are very different and thus not particularly comparable. Another technique, often utilized by misguided principals, is the "sell yourself" approach. Their idea of interviewing a potential teacher is to sit back silently and wait for the applicant to carry on a monologue that will convince the interviewer to "buy" the candidate. The problem here is that many perfectly fine applicants have been led to believe, and rightly so, that it is poor form to be overbearing and egotistical in the interview situation and that it generally behooves the candidate to lie back a little and let the interviewer take the lead in setting the direction of the conversation. Thus an impasse is reached, and the interviewer may well end up hiring the applicant who is most inclined to brag rather than the one who is best equipped to teach.

The best advice for the interviewee is to be aware that interviewers sometimes attempt to evaluate candidates based on the wrong characteristics or to evaluate the right characteristics by using the wrong methods. Once you are aware of these unfortunate tendencies and alert for their manifestations, you will be better able to respond so as to minimize their adverse effects on the interview's outcome.

Sometimes, in fact, you will be able to turn these quirks to your advantage. For instance, if you suspect early in the game that the interviewer relies largely on gut instinct, you will want to concentrate on establishing rapport with him or her so that a feeling of friendliness and mutual understanding pervades the interview. The greater the rapport you are able to establish with this interviewer, the higher your chances of success will be, regardless of your actual qualifications for the job.

TIPS   Arrive approximately fifteen to twenty minutes before the interview and take a moment to relax before you enter the office where you report for interviewing. It is often advised to go to the washroom and straighten up beforehand.

If you are unfamiliar with the area, travel to the school the day before.

Knowing the School District

In the early stages of the job-hunting game, the extent to which you will be able to research the prospective employer will depend on many variables: the way you heard about the job, the amount of advance notice prior to the initial contact, and the accessibility of information through printed material or personal contacts. Obviously, if you are applying in answer to a blind want ad (where the name of the organization is not given), you will not be able to bone up on the school until they answer your initial letter. At the other end of the spectrum, if you have utilized the do-it-yourself approach to design your own job with a specific school, you will have ample opportunity to learn everything there is to know about the school before you ever breathe a word to your, hopefully, "future boss." The best advice we can give is this: the minute you know the name of the district that is hiring, take the time to do a little research on them before you proceed with the next step. If the school's or district's name is known to you, learn all you can about its organization before writing or calling for an interview. (Naturally, you will not want to spend an inordinate amount of time doing your research, because then your application will be so late that the job may already be filled. But a few hours, or even a day or two, probably won't make much difference in terms of consideration of your resume, and it can make a great difference in your ability to appear knowledgeable.) If you are answering a blind ad and your resume prompts the district office to call you, you will know the name of the district at that time and can do your research prior to the actual interview.

The same rule holds true for the specific school within the district where you will be interviewed and for the person who will be responsible for deciding whether or not you are the person for the job. The sooner you know these details and the more you know about them early in the game, the better prepared you can be to put your best foot forward during the various stages of the employment process. What kinds of things should you know about the district? As much as you can learn, in the time available, from as many sources as possible.

1. What can you learn about the area the district services, the school board, and the types of students enrolled?
2. How is the district structured, and how does the hiring department or division fit into this overall structure?
3. Is it a rapidly growing district that must look outside the area for people at all levels?
4. Who is the superintendent?
5. What major problems or changes face this district now or in the foreseeable future?
6. What can you learn about the person who will interview you?
7. Does this individual have the final authority to offer you the job?
8. What types of employees does this district prefer to hire?
9. What specific skills, beyond those specified in the ad or job description, is the interviewer apt to be looking for?
10. Does the district prefer to hire individuals who live in the district?

There are many sources of such information, depending upon the size, importance, and location of the district. If you know someone who already works for this district, they may prove an excellent source of information about the schools in general and an invaluable source for information about the specific job opening, department, and individual who will do the hiring. Local newspapers can also be a valuable source of information. Back issues may contain detailed descriptions of the district's establishment, subsequent expansions, and problems it has encountered. Principals, school board members, and superintendents may have been described in the local paper at the time they were hired or promoted. Look further to see what types of employees the school or district is hiring at various levels. Sometimes hiring patterns can provide a great deal of information about the extent and nature of expansion within an organization. Literature distributed by the district itself can be a good source of information. Even though such literature is apt to be biased, it will give you a picture of important issues in the district.

If you are working through an employment or placement agency or through a state or federal job-service organization, the agent should be able to help you do your research. Placement centers at colleges and universities also have access to this kind of information. But even if you are working on your own, a little effort and ingenuity should unearth some valuable information about the district in question. There will inevitably be times when you just don't have enough advance warning to prepare yourself by doing this sort of research. And you can't do much if, at a convention, you see that a district you never heard of has a booth set up for interviewing and you decide on the spur of the moment to talk to them. If these situations arise, the best you can do is to explain candidly that you don't yet know much about the organization but that you intend to learn all you can at the earliest opportunity. Under these circumstances, in fact, most interviewers will be happy to tell you a little about the organization and to give you brochures or other information on the spot, so that you can prepare yourself for possible future interviews with them.

School Information Guidelines

The school district office personnel, school secretary, the department chairs, and officers in the teachers union may all have information that could help you understand the politics of the school in which you hope to work. Be nice to them, and if you can spend time with them and encourage them to enlighten you, you will know what you are getting into and be better equipped to find your role in helping the district. You may want to try using the School Information Guideline (Figure 5.1) to help you gather information.

TIP   Check in the phone book to find where the school district's main office is located and you will find some useful information that will help you in the interview. Use the School Information Guideline to help you gather information.

Ever wonder what happens when you send your resume and application materials to the schools? Figure 5.2 lists what often happens with your job application material once it reaches the schools.

FIGURE 5.1.   School Information Guideline

Places to Contact

A.   School District Office
    educational policy
    yearly budget
    school board meetings, times and place

B.   School Secretary
    student handbook
    teachers handbook
    list of current staff
    policy book
    school calendar
    parent newsletter
    student newspaper
    map of the physical layout of the school

C.   Department Chair, or teacher in the school with inside information
    important issues
    materials such as text and curriculum guides
    school/department power structure
    newly developed programs and positions
    current grants received

FIGURE 5.2.   What Principals Usually Do with the Material You Send

First	Each applicant's teaching credentials are rated.
Second	Letters of reference are analyzed.
Third	Individuals who appear highest in the combined areas are called for a preemployment interview (often over the phone).
Fourth	A few of the most qualified interviewees are called back for a more in-depth interview.
Fifth	Top qualifiers may be interviewed by a subject-area panel.
Sixth	Top candidate before final hiring may be interviewed by the school board.

Looking and Acting Like a Professional Educator

A prospective employer will begin evaluating you the moment you step into the room for your interview, and these first impressions will be based largely on the way you look and act. In these early stages, then, the interviewer's assessment of you will be based on subjective and emotional criteria. And even though this early opinion may have little or no bearing on your qualifications for the job, it will continue to color the employer's evaluation of you throughout the interview.

First impressions, then, are critical. We won't dwell on the point too extensively here, since there have been reams of material written about the subject, and besides, common sense will take you a long way in this area. However, a brief review of some of the characteristics that contribute to that all-important first impression is warranted.

Dressing and Grooming

The first thing an interviewer notices is the overall physical appearance of the candidate, including the manner in which he or she is dressed. The best rule of thumb is to dress for your job interview as if you were already employed in the position you hope to be offered. Also remember some of the stereotypes of teachers or principals. Dressing to look like society's ideal perception of a teacher can give you a leg up. This is a subtle way of showing interviewers that you can "look the part" for the job. Although interviewers may not be consciously aware that you are dressed in this way, it will be easier, later, for them to visualize you on the job.

Remember, education is a conservative field so it is better to dress a bit on the conservative side. Even in this age of denim, a sport jacket and tie for men or a tailored dark dress or suit, which is not too short, for women is never in poor taste. Common sense will tell you to avoid clothes that are flashy, gimmicky, faddish, provocative, or overly dressy, frilly, or not pressed. Sequins, green hair, plunging necklines, running shoes, and T-shirts with cute sayings are out of the question.

A mistake often made, especially by college students and other young applicants, is to dress in a manner appropriate to what they *are* rather than what they *want to be*. The best-dressed students on campus may wear T-shirts and running shoes—but the best-dressed administrators don't! Anything you can do to help the employer visualize you in the job you ultimately hope to obtain will be to your advantage. Anything you wear that makes you look too young, too sloppy, or too frivolous to be professional will work against you.

Lest anyone take us too literally, we are not advocating that you go to ridiculous lengths in trying to "look the part." Stick to appropriate street attire and to what is reasonable for your age and sex. It is not necessary to wear designer clothing, but it is important to be well groomed.

Cleanliness and good grooming are at least as important as the style of clothing you select. The most expensive, well-tailored, and appropriate clothes create an unfavorable impression if they are dirty, wrinkled, or ill fitting. And clothes will hardly be noticed if your fingernails are dirty, your beard ragged, your hair greasy, or your shoes muddy and scuffed. Neatness and cleanliness are important everywhere; they are especially critical for jobs in which an individual is seen as a role model to others.

Bad habits such as gum-chewing or head-scratching can also lead to an overall impression of sloppiness or nervousness and should be avoided during the interview.

TIP   Remember that you want to portray respect and confidence in your interview.

Mental Attitude
(or Things That Can "Underwhelm" an Interviewer)

Just as interviewers will be forming impressions based on your general appearance and dress, they will also be forming impressions about your personality and attitude right from your opening words. If you appear excessively timid or frightened or if you act as if you have a chip on your shoulder, this impression will stay with the interviewer even though you become friendly and relaxed as the interview progresses. A person who acts like a frightened little mouse will plant serious doubts as to his or her ability to deal with students. One who is overly aggressive and boastful will lead the interviewer to wonder what defects this manner is designed to hide. And the person who is sullen and seemingly unwilling to impart any information will be pegged by the interviewer as uninterested in the job or downright uncooperative and unpleasant. The latter applicant will also be at a disadvantage because teaching usually requires a high degree of verbal fluency.

The most beneficial attitudes you can convey during the interview, through words and actions, are respect for the interviewer without fear of his or her power; self-confidence without cockiness; a spirit of cooperativeness; friendliness without gushiness or overfamiliarity; sincerity; honesty; and genuine interest in the job and the school. Rudeness, inattentiveness, and challenging the capability of the interviewer are out of the question.

In addition to listening to your words, the perceptive interviewer will be alert to various other signals that offer clues about your attitudes and feelings. In recent years, the study of body language has become widespread. Though this study has become quite complex and sophisticated in many cases, *body language* is really just a new name for a phenomenon that everyone recognizes—the communication of thoughts and feelings through our actions and movements.

It is important for the applicant to be aware of what he or she is communicating to the interviewer in this nonverbal manner. Rapid eye movements, a cowering posture, clenched fists, halting speech, or a highly pitched voice may all communicate your nervousness or fear during the interview. Leaning back in your chair, on the other hand, indicates relaxation, though an overly casual posture may signal excessive cockiness or insolence. Sloppy posture may indicate to the interviewer that you are a person who could be slipshod in your work habits as well; excessively stiff, prim, and proper posture, on the other hand, can reflect timidity or lack of flexibility. If you repeatedly glance at your watch or at the door, you will be telling the interviewer that you are bored or in a hurry to leave.

During the interview, try to avoid such distracting habits as playing with a pen or pencil; shuffling papers; drumming fingers on the desk or chair arm; scratching or rubbing your head, ear, or chin; playing with a strand of your hair; popping your knuckles; nodding your head too often; or any other type of behavior that would fall into the general category of nervous movement or "fiddling around." Such movements are annoying. They may indicate to the interviewer that you are nervous, lack self-confidence, or are simply uninterested in the interview. In any case, they seriously distract the interviewer from listening attentively to what you are saying and hamper your attempt to sell yourself and your qualifications. In short, the communication process suffers just at a time when you need to establish rapport and focus the undivided attention of the interviewer on what you are saying.

Another important aspect of nonverbal behavior is the establishment of eye contact with the interviewer while you are communicating. This does not mean that you should stare relentlessly, "boring holes" with your eyes, but simply that you should make direct eye contact from time to time as you would while communicating face-to-face with a friend. Avoidance of eye contact, for instance, by staring down at your lap or at a spot on the desk, can indicate excessive timidity or even lead the interviewer to suspect that you have something to hide or are afraid to tell the truth about your background. Looking elsewhere—out the window, for instance—gives the impression of lack of interest in the interview.

In summary, then, use common sense to make the initial impression a good one. Show up for the interview neatly and appropriately dressed; sit with correct but not rigid posture; and be sure your motions, your tone of voice, and your actual words communicate a friendly, respectful, honest, self-confident, and cooperative mental attitude.

TIP   If you have any of these fidgety tendencies, you might consider videotaping or audiotaping a practice interview to help you "clean up" your act! It may also be helpful to ask a friend or family member to watch you carefully and see if any habits such as these—of which you may be unaware—exist.

Developing a Useful Portfolio

As you get ready for the interview, developing a portfolio will also help you present yourself well. The portfolio for teaching is usually a systematic collection of data that documents and highlights an individual's work in the field. For example, it may contain evidence of an individual's skills, strengths, talents, experiences, and professional growth over time. For individual educators, it is a tool to help evaluate themselves or to help sell their strengths and abilities to an interested school district.

Two Basic Purposes of Portfolios for Educators

In the field of education a portfolio has many different purposes. An educational portfolio may be a tool for assessing your teaching skills, or a job search tool.

Educational portfolio assessments may be used in multiple ways. The assessment of education students who are learning to be teachers will probably come first. But you may also find districts that use a portfolio as an assessment device to verify their experienced teachers' progress for the purpose of reward and renewal. Both are valuable methods of evaluation although the purposes are different. It has become increasingly common for a portfolio assessment of education students who are learning to be teachers to be required by colleges before an education student can be certified for teaching in any area. Students may be asked to use their teaching portfolios for proof of their attainment of teaching competencies in their field. These competencies are often tied to state departments of education requirements.

The assessment of an experienced teacher's progress for the purpose of reward and renewal is obviously important to teachers who want to make financial and academic progress on the job. Whether the goal is to prove accomplishments for the school's yearly renewal process or for salary increases or merit pay is unimportant. It is still an excellent format to use to increase lifetime learning and to further develop into a reflective practitioner.

The usefulness of the portfolio in the job search is dependent on the time and energy put into the portfolio's development and the knowledge the applicant has about the specific job. Just as you evaluated yourself for your resume and interview, you can take your evaluation one step further using the portfolio. After discovering the needs of the district, applicants can highlight portfolio materials that display their skills in particular areas.

A good way to begin the portfolio development process is by keeping a file of especially good projects, research papers, units, and lessons you have done. Then you might keep a journal of your accomplishments and insights so as to help you grow as a teacher or administrator and to help you pinpoint and display your strengths. The contents of your file then can be used as evidence in the appropriate sections of your portfolio. Next the contents of your journal can be used to help you remember and enumerate the exciting "ah ha" moments you had in the classroom.

Building Your Portfolio for Presentation

Portfolios have been made out of everything from large box files to briefcases. Unfortunately, some of these portfolios are more cumbersome than most interviewers would want to deal with. The most obvious vehicle in which to build a portfolio is the three-ring binder. (This is the preferred format for an interview but other formats are acceptable as well.) These come in many different styles and you must use common sense about which best represents you and what you can afford. We remember a well-meaning teacher's portfolio that looked like a child's notebook, rendering it too cute to take seriously. We have also seen a beautiful leather notebook that was so expensive-looking that it got stolen off the professor's desk. (Please guard these materials wisely.) The most important ingredient in the portfolio is what's inside. So be sure your portfolio is large enough to hold your materials, yet small enough to not be too daunting for an interviewer to approach. Portfolios can also be developed in expandable files or on a computer disk or CD-ROM. A portfolio on the computer can open up a whole new way of interesting people in your skills. Think of the value of being able to sell yourself on the Internet to school districts across the world!

It is imperative that the job-seeking portfolio be very easy to read and very easy to access. You want to be able to get to the appropriate spot and find your materials with a minimum of hassle and delay. Therefore, your portfolio organization should be very logical and simple. You will need dividers to keep different sections separate. Many people use see-through plastic sleeves to protect and highlight important materials. Most individuals use themes to organize their portfolios (Figure 5.3). However, it is possible to organize your portfolio according to time instead of themes. Find the system that works best for you.

What a Portfolio Should Contain

Usually a portfolio has information in basic areas such as teacher preparation, teaching methods and strategies in the classroom, professional development, communication skills, and perhaps diversity skills. You might use the sections already provided in your college or university assessment portfolio for your job-seeking portfolio or you might use some of these portfolio sections to give you ideas about possible subtopics under each heading.

How Will the Portfolio Be Used?

Interviewers in the field of education are becoming increasingly accustomed to being presented with portfolios. Many candidates try to sell their attributes and skills during interview sessions by using portfolios to support their claims

FIGURE 5.3.   Suggested Portfolio Sections

Teacher Preparation
resume

certifications/licenses

transcripts

reference lists

personal philosophy of education

Teaching Methods and Strategies in the Classroom
student grading system

classroom rules/discipline procedures

sample units

related lesson plans

related pre- and posttests

student work sample

peer assessment of teaching

students'/parents' letters of support and appreciation

Professional Development
additional course work

workshops

in-servicing

professional meetings and conferences

professional writing

professional presentations

educational organization membership
    and involvement

Communication Skills
parent communication system

(class/parent newsletters)

colleague communication systems

teacher/parent conferencing

teacher/student conferencing

teacher/student journaling

(continued)

FIGURE 5.3. Continued

Diversity Skills
special diversity training
diversity practicum work
diversity assignments
strategies for learners of all cultures
second language skills

of competencies. The portfolio can be an invaluable tool in helping you as an interviewee answer queries and back up your responses with examples. They are also useful to the interviewers because it is often easier for them to evaluate your classroom management system, for example, when it is there in front of them to peruse.

Educators going through the interviewing process often report that they appreciate being armed with a large "cheat sheet" that can jog their memory when they are asked difficult questions during the interview. (This really isn't cheating; it is actually being well prepared.)

When interviewees are asked to describe their personal philosophies of education in high-pressure situations, which interviews may be, many individuals find it difficult to know where to start without some written cues. Even if they don't need to look things up when answering questions, it's comforting to know that they have the information at their fingertips in case they need it. If you have nothing to hide, show your work with pride. Good luck!

TIP Remember that the people who interview you may be visual learners, and your portfolio could be invaluable in helping them evaluate your ability to teach in their schools.

CHAPTER

6 Interviewing Strategies and Systems

This chapter tells you in detail how an interviewer interviews. Read as much as you feel will be helpful to your situation.

OUTLINE

Part F.   Is the Interviewer Interested?

Part G.   Frequently Asked Questions
                 Possible Answers to Interview Questions

COMPETENCIES COVERED IN CHAPTER 6

Part A. The Interview Profile
   1. What is the basic outline of an interview?

Part B. The Various Purposes of Interviews
   1. What is the screening interview?
   2. What is the get-acquainted interview?
   3. What is the hiring-decision interview?

Part C. Communication in the Interview
   1. What are the barriers to the flow of communication I need to avoid?
   2. What should I consider in the area of verbal communication?
   3. What's the best use of language and vocabulary?
   4. What about nonverbal communication, eye contact, and body language?

Part D. The Cone System of Interviewing
   1. What kinds of interview techniques might I run into?
   2. What are techniques an interviewer might use to probe for depth information?
   3. How might a good interview be developed?
   4. How can I swing with the system?

Part E. Varied Approaches to Interviewing
   1. How do untrained individuals approach interviewing?
   2. How can I handle these different interviewing styles?
       The application reader.
       The supersales person.
       The amateur psychologist.
       The multiperson interview.

Part F. Is the Interviewer Interested?
   1. How will I know if the interviewer is interested?

Part G. Frequently Asked Questions
   1. Could I answer any question that is thrown at me?
   2. What are possible answers to frequently asked questions?

CASE STUDY AND JOB PROFILE

Jack Jones, the principal at Sauk Dale School, is going to interview Bette Jackson, one of the four individuals selected by the district personnel director as having the best credentials to fill the new fourth/fifth grade integrated classroom position. Bette is an experienced teacher whom he met for just a minute yesterday. When the position opened, Jack outlined the following characteristics as those he most needed in a teacher in his new fourth/fifth grade program.

The following is the job profile for the fourth/fifth grade teacher. Following the profile is the interview Jack had with Bette the day after her initial interview with the district personnel director.

Fourth/Fifth Grade Elementary School Teacher Profile
Personal characteristics necessary for job success in this position:

   a. High energy level—willingness to attend frequent after-school meetings and handle the high stress level of serving a heterogeneous population
   b. Interpersonal skills—ability to communicate and feel comfortable with children, parents, and other staff members constantly in your room
   c. Listening, counseling, and negotiating skills—essential with the mixture of students and staff sharing a small space
   d. Fairness—firmness and understanding required
   e. Dedication to teaching—committed to developing young children's ability to cope with the world they will live in

Fourth/Fifth Grade Elementary School Teacher
Sample Interview

JACK: Ms. Jackson, I'm Jack Jones. It's nice to see you again.

BETTE: Hello, please call me Bette.

JACK: Fine, Bette. Call me Jack. If you don't mind, I'd like to be informal.

BETTE: Fine, I'd like that too.

JACK: Yesterday we were introduced after your initial personnel department interview. I'm pleased you could come back and interview with me.

BETTE: I'm pleased to be invited back.

JACK: As you heard yesterday, we are very excited about our new fourth/fifth grade integrated program. The candidate who ultimately fills this position will play a key role in its success. Could we start by having you talk about the discipline system you used at the Elm Elementary School?

BETTE: Well, my system is rather complicated. Should I begin by discussing my philosophy of discipline in the classroom as a whole?

JACK: That would be a good place to start, Bette.

BETTE: When I got my first job at Elm Elementary School twelve years ago, my discipline approach was very simple. I told everyone my rules and what was expected of them, and rewarded the good performers and disciplined the laggards. That worked well for a time, but as the children coming into the classrooms changed, I realized that I needed to individualize my expectations and my system of rewards and punishments.

Now, my discipline system is tailored to each child's needs, as are my academic expectations. I can show you in my portfolio some sample behavior programs for my individual students.

JACK: Why do you think the children changed?

BETTE: I feel children have been raised differently and society as a whole has changed. Children seem to follow rules much better when they feel they have a voice in the rules and learn that they need to take responsibility for their behavior. When following rules is approached as a learning situation, I find the children work with me and each other to solve behavior problems and they are much better able to self-manage their behavior and their academic work.

JACK: That sounds very exciting. Can you describe your teaching strengths?

BETTE: Well, I am very fortunate that I have the ability to understand children. I am able to immediately sense if they are happy, sad, angry, scared, or insecure, and therefore I am usually able to comfort them and help them find their own security so that they can concentrate on doing their best work.

JACK: Can you tell me about areas you would like to improve on?

BETTE: Well, because I am so sensitive to their needs, I feel their struggles deeply, so I need to constantly strive to encourage them to stretch and grow, when I am tempted to baby them and do things to "help" them reach their goals.

JACK: I can certainly understand that struggle. Do you think you have the energy to deal with a combination classroom, with students with disabilities integrated into it?

BETTE: Well, Jack, I have always been a person who likes to give my all, and I like a challenge because it keeps me excited about what I'm doing. The most pleasurable and rewarding classes I have taught have been the ones with varied and unusual children in them. I have heard about how well your experimental first/second grade room has worked, and I feel it's a tribute to the excellent staff and leadership here at Sauk Dale School. I think my experience working with students with disabilities in Georgia and my ability to relate to children at multiple levels will help me be successful in this innovative new program.

(After another twenty minutes of interviewing, Mr. Jones further described the position and then explained the next step in the interview process.)

1. What did you like about the way Mr. Jones treated Bette?
2. What did you like about the way Bette answered his questions?
3. Do you think Bette is a strong contender for the job?

To put your best foot forward in the job interview, you will want to determine exactly what the interviewer is trying to do and how he or she is attempting to do it. In other words (to borrow an old football cliche), to establish a defense, you must understand the offense. Think of the interview as a football play, with the interviewer as the team possessing the ball. You both know that the ultimate objective is to score (or, in this case, to fill the job). So you know the interviewer will be heading toward that goal in one way or another. But is this a short play, designed to set up the big play? Or is this the bomb? Will the interviewer run or pass? In which direction will he or she go, and how many fakes will be thrown in to keep you off your guard?

Until you know something about the play the interviewer is setting up, you will be unable to make a decision about where you, the defense, should move. But if you're familiar with the basic offensive plays, you may be able to narrow down the possibilities and anticipate the movements soon enough to keep up.

There is a basic fallacy in this analogy, so we will not carry it much further. The difference is that you want the other team (the interviewer) to score (fill the job). You just want it done in one particular way—by hiring you instead of someone else. So you are not exactly on the defense, and, in fact, it will usually be to your advantage to help the offense along while attempting to steer it in the direction you want to go.

As we discussed earlier, the odds are growing every day that the interviewer you meet will have had some training in interviewing techniques and strategies. In this chapter, we'll take a look at some of the approaches he or she may be using as well as some of the problems you may encounter with untrained or poorly trained interviewers.

The Interview Profile

Good interviewers generally have a plan set up for the interview that divides the session into distinct sections, each with a purpose of its own, and specifies the approximate amount of time to be spent on each portion. Such a profile for a thirty-minute interview might be as follows: An *introduction,* with ice breaking, which lasts around five minutes. The *structure,* or road map, which describes where the interview is going, lasting approximately one minute. The interview *body* or assessment continuing for about fifteen minutes followed by the *influence and sell* portion of the interview lasting approximately seven minutes. A good interviewer will end the interview with a *summary and close,* which generally takes approximately two minutes. See the interview profile in Figure 6.1.

FIGURE 6.1.   The Interview Profile

	30 Minutes
Introduction	5 Minutes
Structure	1 Minute
Body (Assessment) academic background work experience special training (service) career goals and attitudes outside activities and so on	15 Minutes
Influence and Sell	7 Minutes
Summary	2 Minutes

TIPS	By knowing what part of the interview you are in, you are likely to be more relaxed and able to concentrate on your answers.

In the introductory part of the interview, you might be offered something to drink. A good rule of thumb is to follow the lead of the person interviewing you. If they have a drink then go ahead, but if they do not we suggest you skip this as well.

The timing, of course, can vary greatly according to the type of interview being conducted, and we will talk more about the various types in the next section of this chapter. Anything from ten to fifteen minutes for a cursory screening interview to two hours or more for a depth interview might be within the normal range. But the stages of the interview will remain about the same regardless of the time allotted for each. Each of these stages is designed to meet some of the objectives of the interviewer.

1. The *introduction* is that period of time set aside at the beginning of the interview for the interviewer to get acquainted with the applicant and make him or her feel at ease. Here, the good interviewer will not be asking questions designed to test your attitudes about work or to measure your skill, but will simply be trying to establish good communications between the two of you. Depending on the personality of the interviewer, you may expect small talk during this initial phase.

2. The *structure phase* of the interview is simply an outline of the procedure that will be followed during the rest of the interview and an estimate of about how long it will take. The interviewer might say: "Well, Janice, I thought we might chat for half an hour or so about your experience and about the job here at Allentown High School. I'd like to spend the first fifteen minutes or so asking you some questions about your background and interests, so we can get an idea how you might fit into our foreign language department. After that, I'll be glad to answer any questions you have about the job or about the school in general." This structure phase is really a courtesy to the applicant and is, unfortunately, skipped by many interviewers. If your interviewer doesn't offer any clues about how long the interview will last or when you are expected to ask your questions, my advice is to (1) refrain from asking about the length of the interview and (2) hold your own questions about the school until it appears that the interviewer has finished questioning you about your background and interests. However, it can be to the candidate's benefit to learn as much as possible about the job specifications early in the interview. So, if there is a lull in the conversation early on and the interviewer doesn't seem to have a clear-cut idea of what should come next, you might slip in a polite question about the nature of the position. This way, if you get an answer, you will be better prepared to gear your responses toward the job qualifications later in the interview. But do this only if you can bring it off without

interrupting the interviewer or appearing pushy. You will have to play this one by ear.

3. The *body or assessment phase* of the interview is where the interviewer will be trying to meet his or her primary objectives—discovering whether you are the right person to meet the needs of this particular job. There are several ways of going about this (some much more effective than others); they will be discussed in more detail later in this chapter. This is also the portion of the interview during which you have the best chance to sell yourself to the interviewer by answering questions intelligently and by offering additional choice bits of information relevant to your qualifications for this job.

4. The *influence and sell phase* is designed to meet some of the objectives of both interviewer and interviewee. This is the time when the interviewer may tell you a little bit about the job itself and, if you appear to be a likely prospect, try to sell you on the idea of working for the district. It is also the time when, if the interviewer plays according to the rules, he or she should ask you whether you have any questions about the job. Try to have a few well-thought-out questions in reserve, but be judicious. At this stage, your questions should indicate an active interest in the job for which you are being interviewed. It is perfectly appropriate to ask about the structure of the department, where the particular position fits, why the position is open and how your skills might be utilized. However, many applicants make the mistake of immediately asking questions that can lessen their chances of being selected. These include any questions indicating that you are eager to avoid work or that you are overly particular about your working conditions or colleagues. This is not the time to ask, for instance, whether you will be able to leave early once a week in order to pick up your child from dancing class. Another question that turns off most interviewers, though it is unmistakably on the minds of most applicants is: "How long is the Christmas break or how fast does the salary scale move up each year?" Seasoned job seekers as well as inexperienced ones often make the mistake of asking about benefits before raising any other questions. When in doubt, begin by asking questions about the school or district as a whole and about the nature of the job that is open. Once mutual interest has definitely been established, there will be time to discuss in-servicing opportunities, insurance, sick leave, and other such matters.

5. In the *summary phase* (which may also be slighted by inconsiderate or untrained interviewers), the interviewer simply summarizes what has transpired during the interview and lets the applicant know what to expect as the next step in the hiring process. If the interviewer summarizes the highlights of your background and experience and you believe he or she has made a major error in interpreting what you have said, by all means offer the correct information—politely, of course. If you are not told when you can expect to hear from someone about the job, it is perfectly

proper to say, "I hope I'll be hearing from you soon." This should prompt the interviewer to let you know how long it might be before you hear anything. If you get no such response, just cross your fingers and hope.

TIP We suggest that you not bring up matters such as vacation and salary unless the interviewer brings them up. They may be a matter of public record.

The Various Purposes of Interviews

For some jobs, especially with smaller school districts, the applicant may have just one interview, and this will be with the person whose responsibility it is to hire a person for the job. But more and more frequently, an applicant will be seen several times within the same district or school consortium before being offered a position. These interviews may take any or all of the following forms.

The Screening Interview

We have touched upon the nature of the screening interview in previous chapters. This is a preliminary interview; it is usually used to weed out the hopeless applicants, so there are a few rather specific questions that are based on minimum requirements for the job. Try to be as precise and factual as possible, since if you get through this phase a longer interview will follow.

In some situations, if you impress the interviewer, he or she might continue with a more in-depth interview. This could be positive, since the interviewer has displayed additional interest in you as a job candidate. "Play the game" and don't let down your guard.

TIP Even if you are offered a job, don't stop your search until you have signed a contract.

The Depth Interview

The in-depth or assessment interview in a multi-interview process is likely to be the longest and most arduous session you face. This is the interview in which your prospective employer gets to the heart of the matter by attempting to measure your degree of skill and training. By the close of the in-depth interview, the trained interviewer will want to come up with an accurate assessment of how well you meet each of the specifications for this particular job as well as how knowledgeable you are about the field in general. Your performance during this interview and your answers to questions will determine the way you are evaluated, rated on each skill and attitude, and ranked against the other candidates. This, therefore, is the time when you must go all out to sell yourself.

To make matters even more uncomfortable for the applicant, the interviewer often throws in difficult questions or hypothetical problems, which you may have no means of answering correctly, just to see how creative or logical your thought processes may be. Or, if you hold an advanced degree in your major discipline, you may be asked to describe your thesis or dissertation research—a question that can be amazingly difficult for candidates who completed this research many years ago and have rarely thought about it since that time. And, as a last straw, the nervous applicant may be faced with not one formidable interviewer but a team or even an entire board that must be "sold." Any or all of these situations can reduce even the most self-assured applicant to a quivering mass of fear. But remember, this is it. So take a deep breath, try to remain clearheaded, and concentrate on the following questions:

1. What is the interviewer probably looking for?
2. What can I tell the interviewer about my training, background, or personal characteristics that will improve his or her evaluation of me in terms of these characteristics? (Try not to be too lengthy or verbose, but do answer completely enough to give the interviewer something to think about.)
3. What can I tell the interviewer about my past teaching that will show them that I have always had the ability to handle difficult students?

The Hiring-Decision Interview

Many times the decision to hire will be made on the basis of the in-depth interview. In some cases, however, the top two or three candidates (as determined by performance during the depth interview) will be referred to the principal for the ultimate hiring decision. This is probably true if the principal who has the final say-so is a general educator and you are being considered for a highly specialized position. In this case, your qualifications in your discipline will most likely be determined during the in-depth interview conducted by the department chair, grade level leader, or individual in the building who will work most closely with you. This person will advise the principal as to which candidates seem to have the technical expertise and experience the job requires and will perhaps recommend which ones would best fit into the department or grade level team. They may then reinterview the few candidates with the highest technical evaluation with an eye toward selecting the one whose work-related attitudes, personality, and teaching strengths seem most in line with broader school or departmental objectives. The candidate may be offered the job at the conclusion of the hiring-decision interview if he or she is clearly the best-qualified candidate with attitudes and goals that fit in. More commonly, however, the applicant will receive mild encouragement but will not be notified of the final decision until later, since there may still be other top candidates to consider.

At the hiring-decision interview, then, your best bet is to try to determine whether the interviewer is a specialist in your field or a general administrator. If the latter, you can be fairly well assured that your technical qualifications have already passed the test, so that you can now concentrate primarily on winning the job with your personality, your eagerness to work, your desire to contribute to the students in the community, and so on.

TIP When you answer questions, take your time and listen carefully to what you are being asked. You may find it useful to paraphrase the question, which can help to keep you on track and give you time to think of an answer.

Communication in the Interview

Too often, interviewers impressed with the need to concentrate exclusively on relevant information will attempt to ensure relevance by firing a rapid series of direct questions at the applicant. These questions often seek factual information and encourage brief, terse responses. Usually, the session takes on a "question, answer, question, answer" format, resembling a verbal test. Not only does this type of interview tend to create stress and uneasiness, but it also prohibits the establishment of in-depth communication, that is, communication on the level at which it is possible for the candidate to go beyond all explanation of *what* has taken place to an explanation of *why* it has taken place and how the candidate feels about it. This is the level of communication that must be reached during the interview if the interviewer is to acquire any understanding of the applicant beyond the bare facts and chronology of background. Communication must be established at a depth that will enable the interviewer to gain insight into the applicants as people—their feelings about themselves and their experiences, attitudes, goals, and so forth.

In this situation both the interviewer and the interviewee face a demanding challenge. They both gain by creating a climate that will encourage a free flow of communication, and this communication must be both relevant to the interview's purpose and at a sufficient depth to go beyond surface types of information. This is not always an easy task, since this level of communication must be established in a very short time between total strangers, but it is not impossible if these parties utilize good communication techniques and remain aware of the mechanisms that can block the flow of communication.

Barriers to the Flow of Communication

The flow of relevant communication on a meaningful level can be impeded by a variety of barriers. These can be set up, either knowingly or unknowingly, by both the interviewer and the applicant. These barriers may crop up in any communication situation, but they are especially prevalent in the context of the interview because of the amount of stress inherent in the process. Interviewers may be under a certain amount of stress because they feel the urgency of selecting the right applicant and then making a good impression on him or her. Usually, though, the applicants feel significantly more stress. Their career and financial security are dependent on their ability to put themselves across to the interviewer in the most favorable light possible. They perceive the interviewer as the "insider," and themselves as the "outsider" trying to get in. More important, they feel that the interviewer has the authority—perhaps undeserved—to make or break their career. Applicants may fear that if they say the wrong thing or make an unfavorable impression in this brief interview, it could have an adverse effect on them for the remainder of their lives. It's little wonder, then, that they may feel they are under almost insurmountable stress, especially if they are very much in need of a job. Some of the barriers to in-depth communication that might occur in this stressful situation are discussed subsequently.

As communicators, all of us have learned patterns and habits of reacting to each other that are not intended to simplify or facilitate the communication process. These strategies may be designed by applicants to protect themselves against making undesirable revelations or admissions. In other words, applicants can fail to communicate properly on purpose, to avoid appearing in an unfavorable light.

Defensiveness also impedes free communication. If applicants feel, correctly or incorrectly, that they are being criticized if attacked by the interviewer, they will counter or defend themselves by resisting this attack. Not only will they resist offering the specific information that would prove the interviewer correct, but they may feel compelled to go a step further by stretching the truth in order to prove the interviewer wrong. This defense mechanism, once activated, tends to carry over to future topics as well. The result is that many applicants, once they become defensive, continue in a pattern of resistance that could interfere with in-depth communication.

Often, communication is also hampered because we hear what we expect to hear, rather than what is actually being said. Experience has taught us to anticipate what we will hear next. We listen only for what fits our purposes, or until we have "classified" the speakers or their remarks in our mind. Probably ineffective listening habits have destroyed the flow of communication in interviews more often than any other single error. If poor listening causes a question to be answered incorrectly or the answer to be misinterpreted, the entire complexion of the remainder of the interview can be changed without either participant realizing what has occurred.

Another listening-related barrier is the listener's investment of emotion and time in the evaluation of the speaker's motives and the adaptability of the message to the listener's needs. Both parties to communication are continually coding and classifying—evaluating, sorting, accepting or rejecting, and assimilating messages. Some of this evaluation process is essential to good listening, but if the listener invests a great deal of emotion in the process, then the flow of communication can be impaired.

Often, the opinions communicated by one person will be influenced by signals that have been picked up from the other communicator. For instance, if applicants perceive an approving attitude, they will tend to repeat and overemphasize the kinds of statements that brought about that approval and avoid expressing feelings that might conflict with it.

Sometimes information may be withheld because of forgetting. This may be genuine forgetting, or it may be "selective forgetting"—the tendency to forget or repress certain things because they are negative and therefore uncomfortable to remember. In the same vein, people may withhold not because they want to, but simply because they are unable to admit it. For example, the applicant may be totally unable to say that a particular job is desirable because it is "close to home and will allow the applicant more time with the family." The individual being interviewed has not forgotten this, knows it is true, and wants to be honest but is unable to make the statement because he or she is reluctant to admit that this is the real feeling. Language difficulties also inhibit communications. The words chosen by one communicator must have the same meaning for the other, or communication will be faulty. In some interviews, communication is tenuous because the interviewee's language is over the head of the interviewer or because words are interpreted differently by sender and receiver.

Although we have emphasized here the barriers to communication that may arise as a result of the applicant's stress, we would be remiss if we implied that the candidate erects all the barriers in the interview. The interviewer is under the same motivational forces that inhibit or facilitate communications and yield distortions. To minimize these barriers, the interviewer must also be vigilant to see that any attempt to distort or withhold communications has been eliminated or reduced. This responsibility normally falls on the interviewer. He or she must try to understand their own psychological make-up and that of the applicant, do their best to relieve the pressures and stress that create barriers, and formulate their remarks so that they take into account any language limitations or sensitivities of the applicant. Ultimately, the interviewer bears the greatest responsibility for the pattern of interaction during the interview. However, as the interviewee it could be helpful to understand some of the techniques that can be utilized in establishing and maintaining a rewarding relationship between the two parties involved.

Verbal Communication

Language and Vocabulary. Because of the symbolic nature of language, it is often a poor substitute for the realities that it attempts to represent. The words we use tend to breed oversimplification and overgeneralization, so that two persons using the same words may be using them to express entirely different ideas. On the other hand, two persons who feel the same way about a particular subject may never realize the similarity because they are using different words to describe their feeling. The difficulty of interpretating another's comments increases as the subjective or emotional content of language increases. This cannot be avoided altogether, but when interviewing, it is always helpful to use language precisely in order to minimize confusion.

During the interview you should also try to avoid using words or phrases that may have a very strong emotional connotation for either party, for instance, words that may make an individual feel sensitive or defensive, such as "born again," "establishment," "lower class," "handicapped," and so forth. The amount of emotional meaning or sensitivity connected with a particular word will vary from person to person, depending on the meaning and experiences that each associates with the word. Obviously, some of the examples just cited would have no emotional connotation at all for certain individuals, while they would have a great deal for others. If an interviewee uses a word or phrase that appears to elicit defensiveness or any type of emotional reaction from the interviewer, he or she should rephrase the statement or comment, using a less emotional word.

As we mentioned earlier, language difficulties can also develop simply because one communicator uses words that are unfamiliar to the other. This can often come about because the vocabulary of the interviewee exceeds that of the interviewer. Recently, an experienced biology teacher talked with a young principal who had just been hired. The biology teacher often noticed that when she answered a question about teaching biology, a puzzled, uncomprehending look came across the principal's face and that he failed to respond. She realized that she would have to word her answers much less technically and answer in a more general way. As soon as she had adjusted her answers, she and the principal began to understand one another, and the interview proceeded smoothly.

Another area that frequently causes vocabulary problems is in the use of vernacular or subject-specific language on the part of the interviewee. This was illustrated during a recent chat with a district personnel director, just after he had interviewed several candidates for a special education position. When asked how the interviews went the personnel director commented: "Everyone I interviewed kept using initials such as IEP, IFSP, ADHD, CD, ED, and DD. They lost me in the first minute." As it turned out, the personnel director had no background in special education and was totally unfamiliar with these terms.

Such use of in-house slang or abbreviations not only makes the applicant or interviewer feel like an outsider—as if he is not quite "with it"—but also leads to misunderstandings if the applicant or interviewer interprets the word or phrase incorrectly. A chemistry teacher who is interviewing another chemistry teacher may use chemical terms, as long as he is sure they are universally used.

Although it is important to avoid talking at a level above the interviewer's comprehension, it is equally important to avoid talking down to or patronizing the interviewer. It would not be difficult for teachers accustomed to lecturing students to inadvertently find themselves lecturing the interviewer. Obviously this is important to avoid.

Nonverbal Communication

Most interviewees, when they consider the importance of communication in the interview, reflect only on the verbal aspects of communication and the problems that language usage may entail. They disregard an equally important mode of communication—the nonverbal mode. Yet quite often, what is communicated nonverbally has a greater impact on the outcome of the interview than what is communicated verbally.

When inexperienced interviewees first view a videotaped replay of themselves in an interview session, they are generally taken aback by their own nonverbal behavior. They discover that they are not the way they have pictured themselves, as far as nonverbal communication is concerned. Their facial expression lines, body movements, and distracting habits appear foreign to them; some actually cannot believe that they look and act in the manner captured on the tape, although the evidence is irrefutable. After evaluating their own performance, it becomes obvious to them that they are doing things in the interview, quite apart from the words they use, that are less than effective in enhancing their ability to communicate.

Generally, although interviewees may be oblivious to the nonverbal clues they may be sending to interviewers, interviewers are very much aware of them, even though they may not be able to describe them in so many words. If an interviewee's expressions and movements convey the message, "I am bored," or "I disapprove of you," the interviewer will pick up these clues and react to them, even if the interviewee's other verbal behavior is contradictory.

Eye Contact. One of the most important aspects of nonverbal behavior in the interview is the establishment of eye contact between the interviewer and the candidate. The interviewer or interviewee can greatly enhance the willingness of the other to communicate freely simply by looking directly at each other as if the subject under discussion is of interest. This is one reason note-taking during the interview is discouraged. Each time the interviewer or interviewee looks down to take notes, eye contact with the other is destroyed. The overuse of the application blank during the interview also interferes with eye contact. Many interviewers, in fact, use the application blank as a crutch, because it gives them something to look at while the applicant is talking. This is a distraction and can only hinder the communication process. A good rule for the interviewee who has trouble establishing eye contact is to remove, insofar as possible, all temptations to look elsewhere. This means eliminating note-taking and perhaps sitting with one's back to the window to remove the temptation to gaze outside while trying to communicate. The interviewee would do well to practice establishing eye contact.

It is possible to carry eye contact too far, although most interviewees err on the side of too little rather than too much. Once in a while, though, a candidate who is a very intense person will establish too much eye contact, so that he or she seems to be staring at the interviewer. In such cases, interviewers may feel that the candidate's eyes are "boring holes through them," and begin to feel extremely uncomfortable because of the intensity of the eye fixation. This also blocks the free flow of communication. Interviewees who feel that interviewers are frequently uncomfortable during their interviews should consider this as a possible cause. Extremely intense interviewees sometimes find they have to moderate their eye contact by forcing themselves to shift their gaze away from the interviewer's eyes or change facial expressions from time to time. It should be stressed, however, that the average inexperienced interviewee most likely has the opposite problem and should be concentrating on looking at the interviewer more often. The trick is to look directly at the person conducting the interview with an accompanying thoughtful or pleasant facial expression, so that the overall picture is of someone who is listening with real interest and understanding.

Body Movements. Body language is also important during the interview. Interviewees who sit too stiffly during the entire session may communicate an air of formality that makes other people feel uncomfortable and inhibited. Interviewees who look more informal and comfortable, without appearing sloppy, invite freer communication. Interviewers may also feel uncomfortable if the candidate leans too far forward, because this may be perceived as a threatening posture or an attempt to become too personal—too "close" to the other person—before they are ready for this degree of proximity. Frowning or scowling can also be threatening. Some interviewees are surprised to learn that they frequently scowl when they are trying to concentrate on the other person's meaning. In the interviewer's eyes, however, the scowl may be interpreted as a sign of disapproval rather than of concentration.

Some actions have definite interpretations in the minds of most observers. These interpretations may be made unconsciously, just as the gesture itself may be unconscious, but their effect on the flow of communication is unmistakable. Some such actions, both desirable and undesirable, are listed in Figure 6.2, with their interpretations.

No doubt you can think of many other examples. Interviewees should try to avoid gestures with undesirable or negative interpretations and increase their awareness and use of the more positive actions.

Note-taking during the interview, in addition to destroying eye contact, can be perceived as a nonverbal threat to interviewers, who are more likely to be wary of what is said if they know it is being recorded. If candidates feel it is imperative to take notes, they should begin by telling the individual conduct-

FIGURE 6.2.   Body Language

Action	Common Interpretation
Offering a cigarette	"Relax."
Leaning back in chair	"I have plenty of time."
Glancing at watch, clock, or door	"Hurry," or "I'm getting bored."
Nodding head	"I agree," or "I understand."
Silence	"I'm contemplating what you've told me."
Putting notes aside	"This is off the record."
Snapping book shut or suddenly folding up application blank	"Let's bring this thing to a close."

ing the interview that they are writing notes to themselves and hope it is not disruptive.

Little irritating habits on the part of the candidate can severely disrupt the flow of communication, especially if these habits are repeated at frequent intervals. Most interviewees are completely unaware of such habits, but interviewers quickly notice them and either interpret them as signs of the interviewee's boredom or become so fascinated with them that their train of thought is lost. In either case, the communication process suffers. Distracting habits that fall in this category often include playing with a pen, pencil, some other object on the desk; shuffling papers; drumming fingers on the tabletop; scratching or rubbing the head, ear, or chin; playing with the hair or beard; popping knuckles; excessive nodding of the head; or any other type of behavior that falls into the general category of nervous movements or "fiddling around."

The Cone System of Interviewing

The Subject of Cones

The cone system—also sometimes called the *funnel system* and a variety of other names—is simply a tool or technique taught to interviewers to enable them to get all the information they need in order to evaluate the candidate in light of the job specifications. A basic understanding of this technique and the philosophy behind it will be invaluable to the applicant who encounters it in the interview situation. Even if you draw interviewers who are not utilizing this system, you will be one up on them if you yourself can bring some of its principles into play.

Question Focus. A cone is really a mini-interview, or one of a number of interviews within the overall interview. The cone takes its shape from the types of questions posed during each portion of the interview.

If an interviewer is using the cone system correctly, they will open up each cone by asking an *open-focus question*. This is a question that is nondirective and simply specifies the broad area that the interviewer wishes to investigate without telling candidates what they are expected to say about the topic. Some examples of open-focus questions are:

1. I see you went to the University of Kansas. Could you tell me about your education there?
2. Would you describe your first job with the Titanic Public School District for me?
3. You seem to participate in a lot of volunteer activities. Would you discuss some of them?

Questions such as these open up the subject area. Like one end of the cone, they are broad and open, designed to encourage applicants to say what they feel is important about the subject. They can't be answered yes, no, or with a single word or phrase, and they do not suggest to the candidate what sort of information the interviewer hopes to hear.

Moderate-focus questions make up the middle of the cone. Just as the shape of the cone is beginning to narrow, so the moderate-focus question is narrower in scope than the open-focus question. However, it still is not a direct question that can be answered in a word or two, or with yes or no. Some examples of moderate focus questions are:

1. Please tell me a little bit more about your student teaching experience.
2. Please elaborate on the math program you used at the Titanic Public School District.

Closed-focus questions are found at the bottom of the cone. These are questions that can be answered fully with a "yes," "no," or a very brief sentence or phrase. Although questions of a closed nature are not generally good for communication, interviewers may need to use them to get small bits of information.

Some applicants find closed-focus questions threatening because they appear to pin the interviewee down by requesting very specific information. However, chances are the individual interviewing you is not trying to trip you up: They are trying to get an answer to a specific question for clarification. Examples of closed-focus questions are:

1. Where did you go to school?
2. Your only outside activity was skiing?
3. Was your first teaching job a full-time position?

TIP Sometimes when closed-focus questions are asked in rapid succession they may make you feel as if you are being interrogated. This is probably not the intent of the interviewer and you can always slow down your responses or give more detailed answers.

As we stated earlier, one cone does not make up the whole body of the interview but merely a portion of the assessment phase. An interviewer utilizing the cone system may use five, six, or more cones—-each designed to investigate a particular aspect of the applicant's background or attitudes—in the body of an interview. In a typical interview, for instance, the interviewer might initiate a cone dealing with each of the following subjects—the applicant's undergraduate education, graduate program, first full-time job, most recent job, and outside activities. If the applicant has had special training, such as Peace Corps service, this could be the subject of an additional cone as in Figure 6.3. Generally, each previous job that the interviewer wishes to explore will be treated in a separate cone. Sometimes, though, an exception is made for the recent graduate who has had only a series of part-time jobs. In this case, the interviewer may choose to lump them together into one cone, which might be opened up with a question such as: "I see you've had a variety of jobs while you were going to school. Could you tell me a little bit about them?"

Most interviewers will not set up a separate cone to investigate the applicant's attitudes or motivations; instead, these are usually ascertained or inferred from information volunteered during cones on background-related subjects. One reason for this is that it is much more difficult to get someone to talk about attitudes than about experiences. It is possible, however, for the professional to set up a cone for the specific purpose of exploring a set of attitudes. Such a cone might begin: "Would you tell me something about your hopes for the future, and

FIGURE 6.3. Education Practice Cones

Cone 1	"You might take me through your higher educational background."
Education	
Cone 2	"Let's spend some time talking about your first job, teaching at Valley High School."
Employment	
Cone 3	"You have had some interesting volunteer experiences; talk about some of them."
Volunteering	

what kinds of things you are looking for in a job?" These attitude-related cones are usually among the most difficult for the applicant. Here again, it really helps to know as much as possible about the nature of the job opening and the school as a whole, so you can tailor your responses to suit the needs of the job. At the risk of being repetitious, I will caution you again to be truthful. You won't gain in the long run by not telling the truth, but you can be somewhat selective about the facts you reveal and you can put a little more emphasis on those that seem to best fit the job specifications while playing down any that don't.

Probing for Depth Information

The probe is the interviewer's most important tool for encouraging applicants to communicate beyond the superficial level. It is used to elicit further information without giving applicants the impression that they are being interrogated. Probes are considered moderate-focus questions because they depend on what has already been communicated and they cannot be answered tersely. There are several kinds of probe techniques, but all are designed to motivate additional communication and to increase understanding between the individuals.

Since effective probes should not reflect the interviewer's bias or modify the original meaning of the question, the most useful probes consist of neutral words or phrases. Many effective probing questions include the words *describe, expand, elaborate,* or words that suggest the same meaning. Some examples of probes of this nature are:

1. How do you mean?
2. Why do you feel that way?
3. I'd like to hear more about that.
4. Would you tell me more about what you have in mind?

Applicants who recognize probes of this kind during an interview will know that a specific topic has caught the interviewer's attention; they will have to rely on their knowledge of the job and their intuition to help them determine what, specifically, the interviewer would like to hear in addition to the information already volunteered.

Another nondirective technique is called the *summary probe.* This simply means that the interviewer invites further communication by summarizing or reflecting what the candidate has just said. A conversation in which the interviewer utilizes this technique repeatedly might sound like this:

INTERVIEWER:	Could you tell me a little about your present job?
APPLICANT:	Well, I've been there for three months, but I'm already sick of it.
INTERVIEWER:	You mentioned you were sick of it. Would you elaborate?
APPLICANT:	You bet. I'll never get a full-time job there.

INTERVIEWER:	You'll never get a full-time job there?
APPLICANT:	No, once you're a substitute there you will always be a substitute; they have a really hard time getting substitutes in the district so they never offer subs a full-time teaching position.
INTERVIEWER:	Then you feel you'd prefer a full-time job even if you had to go to a different district?
APPLICANT:	Definitely!

The assertive phrase (e.g., "I see" or "um-hm"), sometimes accompanied by a nod of the head, can also serve as a probe. In fact, even dead silence (often known as the pregnant pause) can serve to elicit more communication from the applicant; therefore, it must be considered a form of the probe. Figure 6.4 may help you visualize the process of interviewing using cones.

FIGURE 6.4. The Cone

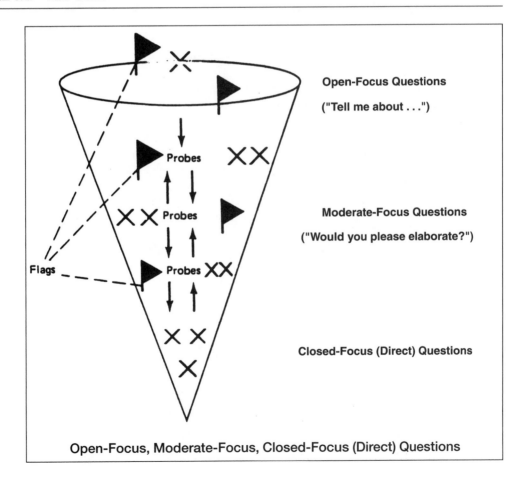

Open-Focus Questions
("Tell me about . . .")

Probes

Moderate-Focus Questions
("Would you please elaborate?")

Flags

Probes

Closed-Focus (Direct) Questions

Open-Focus, Moderate-Focus, Closed-Focus (Direct) Questions

TIP
TIP   When you realize you are being probed further, think about what the interviewer is trying to discover.

Swinging with the System

Now that you understand the cone system, you are ready to examine some specific ways in which you can utilize this knowledge to your own advantage during the interview.

First, we believe that the candidate who encounters an interviewer using the cone system (or some similar nondirective, guided approach) is fortunate. Used correctly, the cone system provides applicants with the best of both worlds: it allows them plenty of opportunity to sell themselves and to mention everything they would like the interviewer to know while also providing enough guidance from the interviewer to keep applicants from going off on unproductive tangents.

No doubt some job seekers will disagree. Those who are extremely glib and persuasive may feel they can do a better interview in a completely flexible interview environment; those who are timid or find it difficult to think methodically may feel more comfortable with a very patterned approach. Nevertheless, if the cone system is what your interviewer is using, you will be looked upon kindly if you help to make the system work rather than thwart the interviewer's every effort—consciously or unconsciously—by failing to cooperate.

A useful mental exercise, prior to any interview, involves thinking in cones. Pose a hypothetical open-focus question about each segment of your background—your education at various levels, each separate job you have held, outside activities or hobbies, and so forth. (If you have been a homemaker most recently, be sure to regard homemaking as a job for this purpose.) Better still, ask a friend or relative to role-play by posing these questions in a mock interview situation. Then decide, for each open-focus question, what points you want to include in your response; practice relating these points to your "interviewer." What are the major accomplishments and attitudes you would want to convey to the interviewer relative to the particular job or activity in question? What aspects of the job or activity would you prefer to omit from your discussion unless questioned point blank either because they are minuses or because you consider them irrelevant?

TIPS   Even if you discover that the interviewer is not using the cone system, your preparation will give you confidence and make you look impressive.

While you are preparing for your interview, think of four or five questions to ask the interviewer so that if asked whether you have questions, you can sound interested and can pose some good questions.

Varied Approaches to Interviewing

There are as many approaches to interviewing as there are individuals who perform the interview. However, some are less and some more effective than others for both the hiring organization and the candidate. We will quickly examine some of the more common of these approaches and then discuss what—if anything—you can do when you encounter them.

The Application Reader

The application reader is an interviewer who carefully goes over the application blank or resume submitted by the candidate bit by bit, asking questions about the answers the candidate has provided on the application form. If this person deviates from the written data, it is to ask brief questions of a factual nature. When the applicant has finished answering a particular question, the interviewer searches the application for the next question. Once the information on the application or resume has been exhausted, the application reader tells the candidate a little about the job and concludes the interview.

This approach may fail to provide the interviewer with much new information on which to base a decision. More important, it could leave applicants with very little opportunity to sell themselves to the interviewer or to establish any kind of rapport.

If you encounter an application reader, you will know it almost at the outset of the interview, and there are two major steps you can take to turn the situation to your own advantage. The first is to do a quick mental review of the information you have listed on the application (or whatever document is being read) and quickly decide what kinds of things you want to say that the interviewer is not likely to ask.

1. What experiences should you explain in greater detail?
2. What facets of your personality would you like to demonstrate, and what attitudes do you want to express?
3. What questions do you want to be asked?

The second step is to become more gregarious than you might ordinarily be in the interview situation and direct the conversation in the way you want it to go. This can easily be done by treating the interviewer's questions—which are almost certain to be direct- or closed-focus questions—as if they were open focus. In other words, expand and elaborate, even though you have not been asked to do so, in order to get across to the interviewer the "selling points" about you and your experiences.

Suppose, for instance, that the application reader peers at you over the top of the resume and says, "You were the head of the music department at your last job, right?" Smile responsively and say something like this: "Yes, and I learned some fascinating things about managing people on that job. When I first took over as department chair, there were two factions that quarreled constantly, to the point where their disputes often interfered with their work. So I . . ." and then proceed to tell a little about how you solved the problem. At this point the interviewer will, most probably, listen with interest to your solution, even though your story may not actually have been anticipated by a specific question.

Of course, you should not chatter nonstop, as this can be extremely disconcerting to the interviewer who sees it as a duty and responsibility to go through the entire application with you, verifying every detail. After all, you do not want to give the impression of being pushy. But most applicants have just the opposite problem; they are too shy and reticent in the interview situation to volunteer any unsolicited information. Just remember, by forcing yourself to be a little more talkative and forceful than usual with the application reader, you will be creating an opportunity to sell yourself that would otherwise be lost. Furthermore, you may also be doing your interviewer a favor for which he or she may be most grateful, since you are shouldering part of the conversational burden.

TIP   When encountering an application reader:

    a. Decide what isn't on your application that you most want to say.

    b. Direct the conversation by expanding closed questions with open answers and elaborations.

The Super Salesperson

The interviewer we will label, for purposes of discussion, as the super salesperson is most often found among interviewers and people with strong, outgoing personalities and a gift for persuasion. Super salespersons greet applicants vociferously, pump their hand, and then may begin to overpower them with information about the job, the school, and the school district. When these interviewers ask applicants questions about their background or goals, they may interrupt with their own opinions, and these generally involve the superiority of the district and why it would be an excellent place for any individual to find a satisfying career.

Super salespersons may not always learn enough about applicants to adequately judge their skills. They are also in danger of not providing candidates with enough opportunity to express their qualifications and goals, because super salespersons can be difficult to interrupt or manipulate into candidate-centered discussions. These interviewers may base the evaluation on candidates' looks, the strength of their handshake, and their superficial personality traits. However, they do one thing that can work in the applicants' favor. They tell applicants a great deal about the nature of the job.

So if you encounter a super salesperson while interviewing, remember that you would be rude to interrupt the sales pitch of the determined super salesperson. However, you can keep your ears open during this pitch, so that you can demonstrate how your qualifications match the job specifications. And if you do not get an opportunity to put in very many words, you can still improve your chances by appearing friendly, outgoing, and truly interested in the sales talk about the schools in the district. If you have done your homework and can add some observations of your own about the fascinating contributions of the teachers or community, so much the better.

TIP   The super salesperson often gives you a great deal of information about the job. So stay alert, listen carefully, and maybe even take notes while looking very interested; and smile a lot.

The Amateur Psychologist

The amateur psychologist may have taken a few courses in basic psychology and has most certainly read articles on the interviewing techniques used by clinical psychologists and psychiatrists. This individual may ask many personal questions that seem to have little to do with employment—some of which, incidentally, are illegal today for this reason. The amateur psychologist is more interested in your personality than in your previous job performance or career goals. He or she is also prone to ask questions to lure you into oversimplifying your own attitudes, such as "If I offered you money, status, self-satisfaction, or security, which one would you choose?" or "What one word 'best' describes you?" You as the applicant probably cannot know how this type of interviewer will analyze responses and behavior during the interview; however, the interviewer is probably trying to see how you fit the personality traits of good teachers and how you are apt to fit into a particular school or community.

It is difficult to advise the applicant about the best method of responding to the amateur psychologist, since the method of their evaluations is unpredictable. It is almost a sure bet that you will not further your cause by becoming defensive or angry, even if the questions leave you feeling as if your privacy has been invaded. On the positive side you may be able to prepare yourself for this type of interview by reviewing the questions at the end of this chapter. These questions are frequently asked by principals and personnel individuals when hiring teachers. It would be in your best interest to prepare some answers to these questions before they come up.

TIP   Although you may be frustrated by the amateur psychologist's personal questions, be sure to keep your cool and answer reasonably.

The Multiperson Interview

In an interview conducted by a two-person team, you will often be able to discern that one member of the team is from your specialty area and the other is from the district at large. If this is the case, the former will mainly be intent on assessing your technical qualifications and skills while the objectives of the latter will center around assessment of your personality and attitudes.

Occasionally you will find that one member of a team is the lead interviewer while the other is there more or less for training purposes. Needless to say, if these two interviewers seem to be reaching toward different objectives, establish rapport with and meet the needs of the lead interviewer first and then continue on, if you have the time, to see if you can uncover the purpose of the other interviewer.

In a board or committee interview, where many fields of interest or many disciplines may be represented, you will have to analyze each question as it is posed, try to discern what kinds of information the person who posed the question is trying to obtain, and then structure your reply to meet the needs of that particular questioner as best you can. Don't try to structure an answer that will be all things to all people. Chances are each person on the board or on the hiring committee has specific questions to ask, and each will no doubt get a turn, so concentrate mainly on satisfying the person who posed the question. Each individual in the interviewing room will most likely vote on the basis of your responses to his or her questions and will often take little interest in the questions asked by others around the table.

In multiperson interviews, some of the same techniques you learned about in our discussion of the cone system can come into play. The principles are pretty much the same if you deal with each interviewer as an individual and concentrate largely on the one who has asked the question under discussion.

TIP   Focus on whoever is questioning you at the moment without worrying about the other people in the room.

Is the Interviewer Interested?

In the mind of the candidate, there is one burning question once the interview has been concluded: "Is the interviewer interested in me?" Although it is not always easy to tell whether the interviewer has been favorably impressed—especially if there are more interviews to come in this particular district—there are some clues you can look for.

Your best gauge for measuring the degree of the interviewer's interest is the "influence and sell" portion of the interview. In general, the interviewer who is favorably impressed will try to "sell" the job and the school to the applicant during this late stage of the interviewing process. This interviewer will tell you that it's a great place to work, that the community is great, that the benefits for employees are good, and so forth. Often the interviewer will also begin to project the candidate into the job. For instance, the interviewer may say, "When you are working here . . ." or "Your duties will include . . ." This sort of behavior on the interviewer's part can often be interpreted as a signal that the assessment is over and that you are the favored candidate.

Unfortunately, one cannot bank too heavily on this interpretation. Highly trained, professional interviewers often deliberately avoid selling a candidate on the job at the time of the assessment interview, even if their reactions are highly favorable. Their reasoning is twofold. First, they prefer to use all the time allotted for this important interview to evaluate the candidate, on the assumption that the best candidate can always be sold later; second, they have been taught that it is inconsiderate to raise false hopes in the candidate if there is any chance, however remote, that another applicant will be awarded the job. For these reasons, then, the very best interviewers may not talk much about the school and its benefits or project you into the job at the time of the assessment interview even if they are fairly sure that they will make you an offer, and they most certainly will not do so if the final hiring decision is not theirs alone.

At the other end of the spectrum, you may encounter untrained interviewers who will go into the "sell" at the conclusion of the interview simply because they don't know what else to do. These persons, likely ill at ease during the interview, often run out of gas before the allotted time is up and launch into a sales pitch about the job or the school in order to conclude the session on a positive note. Here again, before you know how much confidence to place in the sales pitch or absence thereof, you must read the degree of sophistication of the interviewer and try to discern whether this individual has the authority to make the final hiring decision.

When all is said and done, unless an actual job offer is extended on the spot, you will not know for sure. Though a good interviewer will give you some idea of a time frame within which you may expect to hear something definite, you will still, no doubt, feel that the nervously awaited phone call seems to be weeks—no, months—in coming.

Frequently Asked Questions

There are thousands of questions that interviewers may ask, but often they ask questions that come up over and over again. First we listed possible questions for you to practice with (Figure 6.5). Then we tried to take the most important questions, those we feel you are most likely to be asked, and we have suggested an appropriate answer (Figure 6.6). Some questions have very broad answers and can only be used as examples so as to give you clues as to what the interviewer might want to hear; but these answers will not work for you unless they fit your situation. Perhaps it would be helpful to glance at the questions first, and then you can look and see how they might be answered.

Some questions may be illegal; however, whether valid or invalid, try answering all of these questions before each interview. You may want to make multiple copies of this section so that you can answer specifically for each teaching position.

FIGURE 6.5.   Samples of Frequently Asked Questions

1. How do you like to see yourself and what are your professional goals for the future?
2. What type of position are you interested in? Why?
3. What qualifications do you have that suit you for teaching?
4. What personal characteristics are necessary to succeed in your field?
5. What position in our school would you choose if you were able to pick freely?
6. What are the disadvantages of the field you have chosen?
7. Do you like working in a small or large district?
8. What do you know about our district?
9. Why do you think you want to work for us?
10. What sort of principal would you like to work for? Why?
11. Tell me how you think children learn best.
12. Why are you interested in our school district?
13. How much money do you hope to be making here?
14. How much by age thirty?   Age forty?   Age fifty?   By retirement?
15. What type of environment do you prefer to teach in?
16. Would you be willing to teach anything in the district?
17. What is the most important thing you have learned from the previous jobs you have held?
18. Are you more interested in making money or in serving others?
19. Would you like to teach by yourself or with others?
20. What sort of teachers would you choose to work with?
21. What have you done that shows willingness to work (creativeness, initiative, etc.)?
22. Are you willing to advocate for your students even if it displeases your superiors?
23. What characteristics do you look for in your best friends?
24. Are you greatly concerned with pleasing other people?

25. What is your major strength?
26. What is your major weakness?
27. Do you like to be on stage?
28. Define teaching.
29. What types of students rub you the wrong way?
30. Do you have trouble being tolerant of people who are appreciably different from you?
31. Which of your teachers had the greatest influence on you?
32. Tell me how a student's home affects them during the day.
33. How did you get along with the other students in your education classes?
34. At what age did you first decide you were interested in education?
35. How do you usually spend your weekends?
36. How did you spend your vacations while you were in school?
37. What kinds of books and magazines do you read?
38. How often do you expect to attend voluntary school functions?
39. How often do you go out? Where do you go, and what do you like to do?
40. Do you think potential employers should consider a student's grades? Why or why not?
41. How did you happen to go to college?
42. Why did you select this particular major (teaching)?
43. If you were starting over again, what major (type of work, etc.) would you select? Why?
44. Do you think you have done the best work you are capable of?
45. Have your extracurricular activities been worth the time you spent on them? Why or why not?
46. Would you be willing to forget all about your education and start over again from scratch?
47. Tell me about yourself.
48. Define mainstreaming.
49. Define least-restrictive environment.
50. Describe how you motivate reluctant learners.
51. Have you had experience with cooperative learning?
52. How would you describe a typical hour in your teaching day?
53. How would you grade a student with exceptional educational needs who is working in a regular classroom?
54. How do you feel about whole language instruction?

(continued)

FIGURE 6.5. Continued

55. Please tell me about your favorite lesson to teach.

56. Please describe what you feel is your responsibility to teach children in the area of morals and appropriate behavior.

57. How do you feel about teachers being required to serve lunchroom or recess duty?

58. If you had a student who was wandering around the class, talking loudly, and refusing to take his seat, what would you do?

59. What do you feel is a fair form of judgment for a child who does not complete his or her homework?

60. Whose job is it to handle discipline in the schools?

61. What is the most important skill you can teach a middle school student?

62. What have you found to be the most effective teaching method for you?

63. What do you feel your role should be in curricular development in your subject?

64. How will you deal with the multicultural aspects of this community, if you teach in this school system?

65. What is the first thing you would do when you get your classroom?

66. Describe what you think is a proper atmosphere for learning.

67. Describe your position regarding failing students versus retaining students.

68. How do you propose to remain current as a teacher?

69. Do you like children (or adolescents)? Why?

70. How important do you think daily lesson plans are?

71. Please tell me about the most rewarding thing that has happened to you as a teacher in the classroom.

72. What is the main purpose of schools in our society?

73. What long-range goals have you set for yourself?

74. What is your greatest strength in the classroom?

75. What is your greatest weakness in the classroom?

76. Tell me your experience with team teaching.

77. How are you able to use computers in your classroom?

78. What texts would you prefer to use in a classroom such as the one we have described?

79. Give me an example of how you would handle a parent who was very upset with you for not giving their child an "A."

80. How do you feel about school choice?

FIGURE 6.6.   Possible Answers to Interview Questions

1. *What kind of teacher are you?*
    Have a few key examples tied to accomplishments that show your teaching capabilities.
    "Because I am a very positive person, I can see the best in all of my students. I strive to inspire my students and let them know they can succeed. Fortunately they rarely let me or themselves down."

2. *What motivates you?*
    "I am extremely motivated by seeing growth in my students, as well as my own personal growth. I love a chance to learn; I am a lifetime learner and encourage all my students to be as well."

3. *What do you not like to do?*
    "I believe it is important to do whatever is necessary to get the job done. When I do run into something disagreeable, I try to do it first and get it behind me."

4. *Would you like to be the principal of this school?*
    "At this time I'd like to be the very best teacher I can be; I'm looking forward to doing that with the help of my colleagues in the district."

5. *Why have you left your present job?*
    We advise you to be positive here.
    "I really liked my old job but I feel a new challenge keeps people fresh, and I want to stay invigorated and enthusiastic about my teaching. I also felt that my personal growth was not on track with some of my longer-term objectives."

6. *Did you increase the Iowa basic scores of your students in your last job?*
    "My students' scores were very high and I was very pleased and proud of the results," or "I am not aware of my students' scores as yet but I am aware of the high degree of success my students have had this year."

7. *How did your principal, coworkers, and students get on with you?*
    How would you describe your relationships with your principal, coteachers, staff, and students? Have some examples of the kind of team player you are. This is a good time to bring up that you are a people person and known for getting along with everyone.

8. *Do you know how to motivate and inspire children?*
    This is a leadership question. Know what it takes to be a quality leader. In preparation, think of your approach to motivating and inspiring your students.
    "Giving a lot of positive recognition to students for their efforts and setting a good example helps me inspire my students to continue to strive. I learned from an excellent teacher the value of being a strong

(continued)

FIGURE 6.6.   Continued

and positive role model for my students, and therefore have always been careful of my personal conduct."

9. *What are your short-, medium-, and long-term goals?*
    Tie your answer to goals that could conceivably be realized in this school. You don't want to get too lengthy, so limit your goals to just the short and medium range. A good answer would include growth in one's job through learning, experience, and accomplishments.

10. *Do you prefer working in a small, medium, or large community?*
    Remember where you are when you answer! You might also highlight your *flexibility* and your strong trait of *adaptability*.

11. *Can you describe something about your teaching that makes it special?*
        "One important key to being a great teacher is to be able to develop fun and creative learning activities while maintaining classroom control."
        You would then describe a very successful creative learning activity you have done with students.

12. *What is the toughest task of a teacher?*
    A good reply is, "I have found that the toughest tasks are also the most rewarding, such as finding the best way each individual student in my classroom learns. And knowing my students well enough to recognize that different motivational approaches work with different personalities."

13. *Why do you want to work for our district?*
    Your reply could be based on their reputation of commitment to children, the community being a nice place to work and grow. Knowing all you can about the district will help here.

14. *Why should we hire you?*
    If you know the job requirements, match up some of your accomplishments and say, "If there are opportunities to do that and more here, then this is a great match between my assets and your needs."

15. *What do you look for in a new job?*
    Be careful! Better know a little about the district and the job you are after. If not, push in the direction of excellence based on former accomplishments.

16. *What was your greatest success?*
    Pick one of your most significant accomplishments in the classroom. If this can be tied to their needs, all the better.

17. *What has been your biggest failure?*
    Try to avoid such things as "Did not get along with my principal or other teachers, did not like the school board policies, too much pressure, too much work, too much overtime, problems of health, personal problems interfering with work."

You may want to discuss this one with friends before the interview. If it can be something you were later able to correct, it becomes a learning experience.

18. *What kind of day-to-day schedule did you have in your last job?*
Stress performance and results rather than reciting what you did minute to minute.

19. *How do you feel about the progress you made in your last position?*
"When I started with the Lakeland School District I was given a classroom of thirty-one third and fourth graders. It was a large class with varied needs but one of the nicest group of kids imaginable. It was a challenge to meet all the needs of that varied group but the students and I worked well together and I was very pleased with their excellent progress by the end of the year, and their above average scores."

20. *What were the most important problems you encountered in your past job?*
"The problem of time; I love teaching and I always wish I had more time with each and every one of my students."

21. *Did you have any frustrations in your past job?*
Here you must be honest and admit frustrations because frustrations are a normal part of any job. Relate some situations you found yourself in that were challenging and then indicate what you did to overcome them.

22. *Tell me some of the creative work you have done with your students.*
Creativity means how you developed an idea, a new theme, or a new program and how it improved the students' learning.

23. *Are you a leader?*
Give examples of how you followed leaders and how you successfully led other people. To be a good leader, you first must be a good follower.

24. *Do you like to compete?*
"Competition is great as long as it does not sacrifice the progress of any of my students. I have found that in a classroom filled with students of varying ability levels I must help students achieve all they can achieve without discouraging them because they cannot all be the best in the class."
This might be a good time to discuss the value of competition within students versus competition between students.

25. *Do you consider yourself successful? Why?*
Think about what is meant by successful. If you have been doing the kind of work you enjoy and have accumulated some accomplishments, this would be a good basis for your answer.

(continued)

FIGURE 6.6.   **Continued**

26. *What can you do for our school that someone else cannot?*
    By now you should know the requirements of the job. Match your
    accomplishments against needs and mix with an interest in what you
    have seen/heard so far. As for the other candidates, you really cannot
    answer, nor would you want to. Answer from what you feel you can do.

27. *What do you like best and least about the position we are trying to fill?*
    You can choose the best part of the job provided it is not something like
    "It is close to my home" or "I can make lots of money." Rather, you
    might say something like:
    "At this point I see no important negatives, that's why I'm so
    interested!"

28. *What was your greatest success?*
    Pick one of your most significant accomplishments tied to the needs of
    the school.

29. *What has been your biggest failure?*
    We suggest you prepare for this by choosing a problem you were later
    able to correct so you can turn it from a failure into a learning
    experience. Also, you can say that you were not ready for the tasks that
    were given you but that, with these learning approaches behind you,
    your handling of those situations now would be much more positive.

30. *What kind of schedule would you like to have?*
    Stress that you would hope to have a lot of time to work with students
    as that is where you feel you contribute the most.

31. *Are you considering any other jobs at this time?*
    If you are, say so—but without detail. If not, say, "I have some
    possibilities that I am considering."

32. *What was the last book you read?*
    It might be a good idea to try to recall a good book you have read lately
    and think about what you learned from it. Be careful. The interviewer
    may have read the same one.

33. *What magazines / newspapers do you read?*
    This would be a good time to mention trade journals that would
    reinforce your interest in the field of education.

34. *How long have you been looking for a job?*
    If it has been a long time, you might mention if you have been doing
    any consulting or other part-time work. If not, tell the interviewer
    honestly how long you have been seriously looking.

35. *Describe your ideal job.*
    Do not forget the requirements of the job at hand. Do not be unrealistic
    here or you will scare off the interviewers. Also, try not to set your

goals too high, or they may get the opinion this position is only a stepping stone to your real desires.

36. *What do you think your references will say about you?*
We advise you to always send your most recent resume to anyone you may use as a reference. Then, follow this up with a phone call about what they see are your teaching strengths. If you have done this, you can honestly say what they were impressed with.

37. *How would you describe yourself?*
Think of your professional goals, keeping in mind the traits you are especially proud of from your self-appraisal.

38. *How would your spouse describe you?*
One would hope that your spouse, if you have one, would be your greatest supporter. What traits from your self-appraisal would most impress him or her?

39. *What would you like to improve upon?*
   "I am always trying to be the best person I can be; because of this, I am working on maintaining a high level of health through good diet and exercise. This helps me keep up with the high-energy students I teach."
   If this answer would not work for you, pick something that will not be a detriment to your ability to handle this position.

40. *How do you spend your free time?*
This is not the time to mention that you like cliff jumping or anything else that may seem highly dangerous, if not downright irresponsible.

41. *What are your major accomplishments?*
Here is a question that lets you mention your teaching successes. Pick the ones that pertain to the job in view.

42. *How many hours should a person devote to his or her job?*
   "I feel it is important for me to devote as many hours as needed to do a job I can be proud of."

43. *What things would you like to avoid in your next job?*
Be careful; it might be a good idea to say something general, such as:
   "As a teacher I am always aware of the sensitivity of adolescents, so I make certain that I push my students to do their best but never embarrass them or let them feel like failures."

44. *How old are you?*
This is an illegal question yet perhaps not harmful for you to answer. If you are offended and do not want to answer, you might try using humor. For example:
   "I stopped counting at 39, just like Jack Benny."

(continued)

FIGURE 6.6. **Continued**

45. *Does your present district know you are planning to make a change?*
   If your district or school does know, then you may say so. However, if
   not, you must be tactful. Your answer could be something like:
   "I've grown a great deal in my present position. I have been there
   12 years and I am ready for a new challenge. At the appropriate time I
   expect to let my district know and, of course, I will do everything I can
   to make the transition as smooth as possible."

46. *Why have you decided to change careers?*
   Your answer could be based on growth, interest, opportunity, or
   your increased flexibility to do what you truly want to do at this time,
   which is teach. It is always an excellent bonus to be able to say
   honestly:
   "I have always wanted to teach and fortunately the opportunity
   has finally emerged for me. I am so looking forward to the fulfillment of
   my dreams."

47. *How many days were you out ill last year?*
   If you have been out a lot, this could be damaging, unless you can
   impress upon the person that it was an unusual, nonrecurring
   incident.
   "Unfortunately, I was out three weeks because of an accident. But
   I maintained daily contact with my substitute and I continued to
   correspond with my students so they knew I was still there to support
   them. The children and I used email, as well as the telephone and mail
   service, to stay in touch."

48. *How do you take criticism?*
   "I take teaching children very seriously and would welcome the
   opportunity to learn how to do my job better."

49. *Can you work under pressure?*
   Here you would do well to think about a time when you handled
   pressure successfully on the job and relate the story without getting
   into too much detail.

50. *Do you have any questions?*
   Now is your opportunity to ask questions about what this job might
   entail.

CHAPTER

7 The Law and the Interview, or I Know My Rights Well

COMPETENCIES COVERED IN CHAPTER 7

Part A. What the Employer Can Demand
1. Is sexual harassment still an important issue in hiring?
2. What should I do if I find the interviewer asking me personal questions about my race?
3. Can my sixty-two years of age be held against me legally when I apply for a job in education?
4. What if I have a severe disability that would not interfere with my being a good math teacher?
5. Can I be asked about my sexual preference or religion?

Part B. Handling Possible Discrimination

1. What if I want to volunteer information that is illegal for an interviewer to ask?
2. Are there any special ways to handle sensitive issues in the interview, such as financial difficulties I have experienced?
3. Are there any guidelines on when I should and should not file a discriminatory complaint?

CASE STUDY

John had always wanted to be a teacher. From the time he was a child he felt that schools needed to be supportive places so that all students could feel free to learn. He was particularly unhappy about his early educational experiences in a school where he felt children, himself included, were not treated with understanding or respect. He could vividly remember being yelled at for not putting things in their correct place when he didn't know where the correct place was. Now that he was a certified teacher, he wanted to make a difference.

But he found himself being interviewed for a job as a kindergarten teacher in the Smithville District, and the interviewer seemed to be trying to talk him out of the kindergarten job and into the sixth grade history position.

It seemed that because of his size, his Native American ancestry, and his sex, he was being led to the other job. The interviewer kept asking him about his childhood and whether or not he grew up on a reservation.

John wanted to talk about his love for teaching and his devotion to young children but the district personnel director seemed to think he would scare kindergarten children and should be teaching "those rowdy middle school children who need a firm hand to keep them in line." John was having a hard time answering all the insensitive, personal, and illegal questions he was being asked, and he was getting angrier by the minute. Just because he had a Native American background did not mean he wanted to teach Native American history.

Understandably, many job applicants who represent minorities—whether they are members of a minority racial or ethnic group, or are individuals with disabilities, women, or members of any other group that has traditionally found it difficult to obtain employment—are worried lest they encounter discrimination during the interviewing and hiring process. Some, in fact, have gone a step beyond merely worrying about the possibility of discrimination; they have learned to expect it.

This chapter is not presented for the purpose of convincing individuals from nonmainstream groups that discriminatory tactics will or will not be encountered during the quest for a job. Neither is it intended to encourage discrimination suits against prospective employers. If applicants expect to find discrimination, they may believe they have found it and imprudently sabotage their own prospects. At the other extreme, applicants who approach the interview with the naive posture that discrimination no longer exists are being unrealistically optimistic. Candidates most likely to survive the interviewing process are those who are well aware of their rights and who know the current trends in the ever-changing struggle for equality in employment. Such individuals are often able to turn this knowledge to advantage, by being prepared to deal with questions or comments that may smack of discrimination while also being mature enough to realize that such questions may reflect more ignorance than prejudice on the part of the interviewer. This is not to say that discrimination is excusable. The opposite is true; however, we want the damage to you to be limited in any way possible.

What the Employer Can Demand

Although the focus of the 1990s was on promotional opportunities and reverse discrimination, unfortunately we cannot say that ethnically diverse males or females or applicants with disabilities will never encounter discrimination during the job search. There are still discriminatory interviewing and hiring techniques being practiced, especially among smaller districts and in areas where the Equal Employment Opportunity Commission (EEOC) has not yet been particularly active. Whether this discrimination is intentional or the product of ignorance, applicants should certainly be aware of their rights and of the recourse available to them for protection against discriminatory treatment.

Let's take a look, first, at some of the major categories of people who are often the objects of discrimination and at the types of preemployment information that the prospective employer should not demand from these applicants. As we do so, however, the reader must bear in mind that the courts are constantly reinterpreting the legality of various preemployment questions and practices. At present, the thoughtless or ignorant posing of an "illegally" worded question, by itself, will not be given a great deal of weight in the courts as evidence of discrimination. Instead the district's past record will weigh most heavily. If it has consistently used employment policies and practices that tend to adversely affect the employment of protected classes, then discrimination is likely to be ruled by the court. Our concern for you, the interviewee, is that you know you do not have to answer discriminatory questions.

Discrimination on the Basis of Sex

One area that has received increased attention from the EEOC is sexual harassment as it applies to preemployment screening. Although there are no criminal penalties or fines that can be brought against violators of the Civil

Rights Act, the law requires offenders to pay compensating damages to those who have been victims of discrimination, including sexual harassment.

The EEOC has issued guidelines that intend to "encourage employers to affirmatively and convincingly inform their employees that sexual harassment is illegal, and to take specific steps to prevent it." This presumably applies to treatment of potential employees during the interview as well as to people who have already been hired. The guidelines assert that unwelcome sexual advances are unlawful, whether verbal or physical in nature, if submission to such advances is either an explicit or implicit condition of employment.

Unfortunately, women in the interviewing situation are subject to many kinds of discriminatory treatment and questioning that stop short of sexual harassment but are nonetheless illegal. Of all the protected classes of applicants, interviewers probably find women most difficult to screen without inadvertently asking discriminatory questions. This is not because most interviewers hate women or consciously underrate them but because they have been conditioned to believe that they need to know certain things about a woman's lifestyle before they can decide whether she is suitable for employment. Some individuals still seem to find it difficult to believe that they can evaluate the candidate without knowing whether she is pregnant, how many children she has, what arrangements she makes for child care, and so forth—all of which are strictly discriminatory lines of questioning. These interviewers fail to realize that they do not really need to know these things; what they really need to know is whether the applicant can comply with specific work schedules and whether she has any responsibilities that could prevent regular attendance at work.

Questions that tend to discriminate against female applicants include those about their current marital status or future marriage plans, those concerning their credit rating or status as head of household, and those relating to pregnancy, plans for future pregnancy, number or ages of children, and child care arrangements. It is illegal to discriminate against a pregnant applicant if she is qualified for the job and if she has her physician's approval for work. It is also illegal to ask a female about her stand concerning women's rights issues.

Questions about the applicant's original name are suspect, whether her name has been changed through marriage or court order, although for the purposes of checking references, the applicant may be asked whether she worked under a different name for the district or school that she uses as a reference.

In general, an interviewer may ask any question that directly pertains to the woman's ability to perform the job (but not whether she has a reliable baby-sitter) or what her long-range career goals may be (but not whether she plans to start a family or how long she hopes to work). Questions that would tend to discriminate against a divorcée or a mother of small children should be avoided, as should any question that would not ordinarily be asked of a male applicant for the same job.

Although most attention has focused on female applicants, males are also protected from sexual discrimination. A male who applies for a traditionally "female" position, such as a kindergarten teacher, is entitled by law to a fair chance for that position, just as a woman is entitled to a fair chance at, say, a district administrator job.

Discrimination on the Basis of Race, Color, or National Origin

Although an interviewer may be unable to keep from noticing that an applicant appears to belong to a minority group or that his or her surname appears to be of foreign origin, the interviewer should certainly refrain from remarking upon this fact or from asking questions that would tend to single out this applicant's racial or ethnic differences. Obviously bigoted questions such as "Why would a black person want to work for our school?" or "Did you know that we don't have any Hispanics working here?" are, of course, inexcusable.

But apart from the obviously discriminatory lines of questioning, there are several areas of inquiry that do not appear on the surface to discriminate against individuals from ethnically diverse backgrounds but that, in fact, have been judged to do so. These include questions about the economic status and credit record of the candidate. Unfortunately, in the past, research reported that minorities as a whole tended to have less favorable credit ratings and lower socioeconomic status than nonminorities—often because they have been the victims of discrimination. EEOC has concluded that questioning along these lines serves to compound the effects of discrimination and have an adverse impact; it therefore should be avoided.

Questions about the applicant's membership in clubs, lodges, and so forth are also considered discriminatory unless the applicant is told to omit mention of those that would indicate religious affiliation, national origin, race, ancestry, or color. Interviewers should also avoid questions about applicants' national origin, length of residency in the United States, commonly used language, citizenship, or other subjects that would require candidates to reveal their race or origin. Applicants *may* be asked whether they speak or write a foreign language (if job duties require this skill); whether they have a legal right to work in the United States; where they currently reside, and how long they have resided in the city or state. The applicant with diverse background should not be required to submit a birth certificate, photo, or the names and addresses of relatives prior to employment; if there is a legitimate need for these, it arises only after the individual has joined the district. Ethnically diverse applicants or individuals with nonmainstream religious or sexual preferences should not be questioned about their stand on civil rights issues or other matters of interest to the particular groups they may identify with.

EEOC guidelines also control testing practices that tend to discriminate against individuals with minority backgrounds. Preemployment tests used to screen applicants should be free from cultural bias and should measure only those skills and traits that are essential to job performance. If possible, they should be validated separately for minorities. Any test that tends to rule out otherwise qualified applicants simply because they represent a particular culture or nation is illegal.

Discrimination on the Basis of Age

Under current law, an applicant who is otherwise qualified cannot be turned down by a private employer of twenty-five or more persons on the basis of age alone unless the applicant is younger than the local age of adulthood or older than seventy, or unless age is a bona fide occupational qualification. Preemployment queries such as "How old are you?" and "What is your birth date?" are illegal in most states; in some, applicants cannot be asked the date of their high school graduation. It is legal to ask applicants whether they are over seventy, provided the district has a mandatory retirement age of seventy. It is also legal to ask young applicants if they have reached the legal age of adulthood in the employer's state (usually age twenty-one).

It is also legal to ask applicants how many years they worked at previous jobs and what their future career plans are, but it is not legal to inquire when they expect to retire. Birth certificates, baptismal certificates, and other records that indicate age cannot be required as a condition for employment.

Discrimination against Individuals with Disabilities

The federal government and its contractors are prohibited from discriminating against any individual who has a physical or mental impairment that "substantially limits" one or more of such person's "major life activities," has a record of such an impairment, or is regarded as having such an impairment. The Office of Federal Contract Compliance Programs has issued regulations that greatly expand the definition to include heart conditions, congenital back problems, epilepsy, terminal cancer, and allergies. More recently, alcoholism and drug addiction have been included. In other words, these and other physical and mental handicaps do not constitute just cause for rejecting applicants *unless* the handicap prevents them from performing the job.

Employers who fall under the control of the Rehabilitation Act cannot ask applicants whether they are disabled, whether they are addicted to alcohol or drugs, whether they have any disabilities or chronic illnesses, or what type of military discharge or deferment they received. It is, however, legal to ask whether applicants have any health problem that would prevent them from performing certain types of work required by the job in question or whether there is any reason that they might be unable to be at work regularly.

Also, the 1990 American with Disabilities Act goes even further to ban employment discrimination. According to Title I of ADA private employers, state and local governments, employment agencies, and labor organizations may not discriminate against job seekers because of their disabilities. Further, it clearly requires nondiscrimination in job application procedures, hiring, advancement, pay, job training, assignments, benefits, and other privileges of employment. It is illegal to retaliate against any applicant or employee who asserts his or her rights under the Act.

This is good news for individuals who have disabilities. However, it is important to know that employers are only required to accommodate disabilities that are known. Any individual with a disability who may need accommodations on the job should probably discuss this during the interview. Here your timing is important. As an individual seeking a job, you may be reticent to immediately demand accommodations. Yet it is wise to inform the school or district, before the first day of school, of the accommodations you may need.

Discrimination for Various Other Reasons

Persons of certain religious convictions are occasionally victims of discrimination. Such questions as "Where do you go to church?" or "Who is your pastor?" are considered discriminatory. Applicants should not be asked to furnish lists of organizations to which they belong unless they are told to omit those organizations indicating religious affiliation. They may also not be asked for baptismal records. Furthermore, it is illegal to make statements to the applicant such as, "This is a Protestant organization." It is also illegal, of course, to discriminate against applicants who have no religion.

Possible discriminatory questions for veterans might include those regarding the type of discharge received from the military or whether they have served in the armed forces of any other country. Veterans cannot be required to produce a DD-214 (military separation record) prior to hiring.

No applicant should be asked questions regarding sexual habits or preferences, roommates, sexual identity, and so forth.

In short, almost any question can be suspected of being potentially discriminatory in nature *unless it relates directly to the applicant's ability to perform the job*. Similarly, any record or document that the applicant is required to submit is potentially discriminatory if it contains answers to questions that cannot legally be asked in the interview. But remember—and we will discuss this more in the next section—that it is not the exact wording of the question but the way in which the information will be used by the employer that is most important in the final analysis.

TIP   Remember, no approach works well unless you are truthful.

Handling Possible Discrimination

Beating the Interviewer to the Punch

If you are among those who often suffer discrimination in employment and you feel that an interviewer may draw unjustified conclusions in your case, it often pays to stick your neck out and answer discriminatory questions before they are posed. Remember, it may be illegal for interviewers to ask certain questions, but it is never illegal for the interviewee to volunteer information that would answer these questions. If you have nothing to hide and you say so candidly, interviewers are likely to be impressed with your candor and your practical approach to a potential problem. Perhaps more important, they may be vastly relieved to learn the answer to questions that they were dying to ask but knew they shouldn't.

We are certainly not suggesting here that you bait interviewers by dangling tidbits of illegal information in front of them to goad them into discriminatory behavior. Some minority groups have planted candidates in interview situations in companies that they suspect of discriminating; these candidates volunteer sensitive, illegal information to test the company's subsequent use of this information and to attempt to trap the company in a discrimination suit. For this reason, experienced interviewers may be suspicious of any highly sensitive information you volunteer unless your manner is very sincere. But if your comments are positive, you may aid your case by bringing a sticky subject out into the open.

Other examples of this approach might include the following statements by applicants who could easily lose the job because of unanswered questions in the interviewer's mind:

> I notice you have very few black principals in this district, and most of your teachers appear to be white. In the army I supervised mixed racial groups and one or two units that were all white, and I found that it worked out very well. The whites accepted me as their superior officer and cooperated with me completely, and we soon forgot that there were any differences.

> As you can see, I'm confined to a wheelchair, but in the past ten years I've learned to cope with that so well that it doesn't hamper my ability to get around or teach. I am medically very fit, except for the paralysis, so my attendance record is excellent. I drive my own specially equipped car and am able to get around in buildings like this very well. And, of course, my previous work record attests to the fact that my disability doesn't affect my ability to be a high-quality teacher.

The entire success of this approach hinges upon the truthfulness of what you say and the candor with which you say it. It doesn't pay to do it halfway, eyes lowered and mumbling as if you have something to hide or to be ashamed of. And be forewarned that once you have broached a traditionally taboo subject, you should be prepared to find the interviewer possibly overcome with curiosity and impelled to ask you more questions about it, even though he or she had no intention of opening up the subject originally. If interviewees bring up the subject themselves, then it is unofficially considered discussible, even though further questioning might be considered illegal or discriminatory in the strictest interpretation of the law.

No matter what you may voluntarily confide to the interviewer, the district has no right to use information you have offered to discriminate against you in any way.

TIP   Instead of letting the interviewer "uncover" areas of difficulty, be up front and let them know; then it is less likely to hurt you.

Handling Sensitive Issues in the Interview

The foregoing advice applies to those with nothing to hide. Now, let's assume for a moment that you do have something in your past or present that you believe could be used to discriminate against you. Perhaps you are a newly divorced father with custody of three children, finding yourself without adequate day care to date. Naturally, you will not be eager to bring up this subject of your own volition. You will try to emphasize your ability to do the job and your eagerness to teach; in most cases questions about your day care situation will not be asked.

But supposing they are. What do you do then? You have three alternatives, depending on the degree to which the information would damage your chances for the job and on the strength of your own personal feelings about providing answers to discriminatory questions.

The first alternative is to offer no information at all and to tell interviewers that they are pursuing an illegal line of questioning. You might say, for example, "I believe it is against the law to ask applicants about their day care situation [or age, or whatever the case may be]." You could also politely inform interviewers that details about your personal life, such as those they are asking, have no bearing on your ability to perform the job. In general, this uncompromising posture could cause you problems. Although it is perfectly true and candidates are well within their rights to refuse to answer discriminatory questions, it almost invariably engenders hard feelings in interviewers. The interviewer may subsequently rate you poorly because you were uncommunicative, uncooperative during the interview, excessively sensitive, or militant, and so on. Or interviewers may cheerfully agree that the question is illegal and apologize for asking it, but chances are that your refusal to answer will make them suspect the worst, either consciously or subconsciously. For while you are perfectly within your rights in not answering, you may have limited your chances of obtaining the job.

The second alternative is to evade the issue by answering the illegal question using an answer to a similar but legal question. For example, if asked a question about day care, future plans, and remarriage, you might sidestep this issue by delineating some of your long-range career goals, with the implication that an uninterrupted career would take precedence over personal plans in the foreseeable future. Surprisingly, this approach often works. In some cases, interviewers hear what they wanted to hear in your response and fail to realize that you have not exactly answered the question. In other instances, your evasive response serves to remind them that their question was in a sensitive and probably illegal area, and they are likely to be more careful about this line of questioning throughout the remainder of the interview. Of course, if they persist in repeating the illegal question, you will eventually have to either answer it or tell them that you are not required to do so.

The third alternative, of course, is simply to disregard the fact that the interviewer's question is discriminatory and answer it directly and truthfully. Then, if your answer would tend to be used against you in the selection process, follow it up with a more positive statement. You could say, for instance, something like the following: "My day care search has been frustrating to date but I have confidence that my search will come to a good conclusion. I am seeking help from the education department at the local college and feel certain that I can find excellent child care before school begins in the fall."

In general if discriminatory questions are asked during the interview, you must find the approach that you can live with best. We realize that it is frustrating and difficult to be asked discriminatory questions in the interview and that it may be very hard for you to treat the questions as if interviewers had every right to ask them. In the long run, only you can decide whether you would rather answer the questions or stand up for your rights and possibly lower your chances.

You will notice that lying is not among the viable alternatives proposed. Although the temptation is great to counter discriminatory questions with fictitious answers, especially in areas where the interviewer will be unable to verify your answer, deliberate lies will rarely help you land the job. Furthermore, they will definitely hurt your chances if you are found out, possibly even resulting in termination after you have been employed. Any district would much rather hear the truth, a polite evasion, or even a blunt accusation that they are asking discriminatory questions.

Filing Discrimination Complaints

Individuals with multicultural backgrounds, females, and individuals with varying sexual and religious preferences as well as those in any other class subject to discriminatory employment practices may at some time or another be tempted to file a discrimination complaint. Whether this action would be prudent or fruitful depends largely on both the blatancy of the discrimination and the stage of the interviewing or hiring process at which it occurred.

Let's consider discriminatory treatment during the interview itself. If a particular interviewer has flagrantly abused or belittled you, made sexual advances, or clearly indicated that a person of your race, sex, sexual identity, or religious beliefs has no chance of being considered, then of course you have a legitimate complaint. That interviewer clearly intends to discriminate against you and in fact has already done so. You must make a conscious decision to enter into litigation, because you may stand to lose more than you gain by making a formal complaint at this time. First, you are almost certain to alienate the district (and thus lose the job) by filing a complaint against it. If you win the case and the school is eventually forced to hire you, you must think about how you would feel about working there under those circumstances? You might decide that a lawsuit is worth your time only for what it can do for those who follow you. These choices are very difficult to make. Obviously much thought is necessary.

Second, at this stage of the game you may have a real struggle convincing the courts that discrimination occurred. Did anyone overhear the interviewer's racist remarks or see his or her sexual advances? Do you know of others who have been similarly mistreated by the same interviewer or representatives of the same district and who would be willing to testify? Or are you totally without proof or witnesses? This is not to say that victims of discrimination in the interview should never file suit against the perpetrator but simply that they should take a good look at the difficulties involved before deciding whether the incident is important enough to justify the difficulties you are likely to endure. Again you must do what you are most comfortable with; no one else can tell you what to do in this instance.

Another aspect to consider is the possibility that the individual interviewer's behavior does not reflect the district's attitudes or policies. Many times, individuals will persist in bringing their own prejudices into play during the interview even though the organization's overall record for treating fairly those outside the mainstream has been good. If an interviewer treats you in a discriminatory fashion during the interview, try to determine whether the district as a whole is an equal opportunity employer with a good reputation among other individuals with varying diverse backgrounds in your community. If so, you might consider calling one of the interviewer's superiors and explaining, calmly and politely, how you were treated. You could explain that you are aware of the district's good track record in affirmative action and that you feel sure they would want to know of any illegal interviewing tactics being employed by their personnel. If the district is sincere in its affirmative action efforts, it will probably be grateful to you for calling up about the matter rather than filing a complaint that would tarnish the entire district's reputation. You may, in fact, even come out ahead, with an offer of a job or at least a promise of special consideration in a second interview.

In the preceding paragraphs, we have been assuming that you are dealing with blatant, intentionally discriminatory tactics during the interview. Yet the fact remains that some of the preemployment discrimination is unintentional. Studies report that as many as 80 percent of interviewers who ask illegal questions during the interview do not realize these questions are forbidden and are not asking them with any conscious intent to discriminate.

For this reason, you may be offered a job by the very same interviewer who treated you unfairly a week ago. If you really want the job, then, examine the interviewer with all the objectivity you can muster before accusing the district of discrimination on the strength of interview questions alone. If the interviewer seemed generally friendly, open-minded, and interested in your qualifications, even though you were asked an improper question, chances are good that the information will not be used to discriminate against you. Similarly, if the interviewer seemed inexperienced or ill at ease, there is a great probability that lack of knowledge and expertise made him fall back in desperation on the old reliable questions about age, marital status, and so forth. Ignorance of the law is no excuse for asking illegal questions, but only you can decide if you want to risk loss of a job by complaining prematurely about discrimination, on the strength of one or two poorly worded questions, when in fact the interviewer had every intention of recommending you for the job.

Usually, then, the most prudent attitude if you are not certain that discrimination is actually taking place is to wait and see. This is especially true when the school involved is known to treat all applicants fairly. In most cases, the time to file a discrimination complaint is *after* you have been rejected for the job *for reasons other than your qualifications* to do the work. This is the important phrase. If you are clearly not qualified for the job, of course, you cannot assume that you were rejected for discriminatory reasons. Even if you were well qualified but there were several other equally qualified candidates in contention, you would have a hard time convincing authorities that you were turned down strictly because you are Hispanic, disabled, or female. It is true that once a charge has been filed, the burden of proof shifts to the hiring organization, and they must prove that they did not discriminate. However, unless you are clearly the best-qualified candidate, the hiring organization can nearly always justify your rejection in terms of a job-related characteristic, showing how you did not quite measure up to the person who got the job, even though some of your other credentials may have been as good or even better. If the district can substantiate its job-related reasons for rejecting you and can also prove that it has a past record of nondiscriminatory hiring, it will be in a strong position to refute your charge.

But if you were clearly the best-qualified candidate and were ruled out strictly on the basis of your race, sex, or other protected category, or if you can show that you were disqualified by scores on an unfair test when your actual job-related qualifications were above reproach, then you may have a discrimination case that is worth fighting for. To find out, call the nearest EEOC office or, if there are none nearby, the local branch of your state job service office. Personnel there will be able to put you in touch with the proper authorities, and you will receive counsel on the advisability of going ahead with a formal complaint. Unfortunately, this can be a long, drawn-out procedure that may severely curtail your chances for employment in the meantime, so you will have to decide whether you want to pursue it or whether you want to continue looking for a job elsewhere. It isn't fair, but unfortunately it is the way things often turn out at present; we would be leading you astray if we were to tell you otherwise.

Questions to Be Considered after Reading This Chapter

1. How would you respond after being asked a sensitive or illegal question by an interviewer?

2. How would you respond if you were told by a school district during interviewing, "We have a number of ethnically diverse principals and supervisors in our district. How would you feel about working for one of them?"

3. Sexual harassment is a very current legal concern in all organizations today. An interviewer asks you: "How would you react to a homosexual proposition by a same-sex supervisor in the working environment?" How would you respond?

4. If you were interviewed by a principal with a severe visual impairment for an open position in his or her school, how would you handle the interview?

   a. What are some considerations you might have?

   b. Is there anything you would be afraid to say?

   c. Would you be uncomfortable in the interview or later working for the principal?

8 Stress and the Job Hunt, or We Can Overcome

This chapter explores a number of topics in the area of handling the stress common to individuals searching for a teaching job and coping with inevitable rejections. If you are interested in these areas, please continue.

OUTLINE

COMPETENCIES COVERED IN CHAPTER 1

Part A. Relieving Pressure during the Search

1. How can I understand and manage the stress that naturally comes from searching for a job?
2. What can I do to get over feelings of hopelessness and frustration?
3. Are there any solutions to the feelings of guilt and inferiority I feel about going back to work or being out of a job?
4. What could help me get past the fact that the perfect job doesn't seem to exist for me?
5. If I am feeling negative and pessimistic can this be turned around?
6. Seeking a job is creating doubts about myself and worries that I will never find a teaching job. What can I do to be sure these feelings don't destroy my self-confidence and hurt my chances of interviewing well?

Part B. Coping with Rejections

1. How can I keep my job application rejections from getting me down?
2. What can I learn from not getting the job?
3. Is there a way to increase my chances for consideration for a job in a district that has already turned me down?
4. Now that I have been turned down, what comes next?

CASE STUDY

Linda Oxford's youngest child was leaving for college in two months. Linda knew she needed to get out and work to help pay for her three children's education and to develop herself vocationally. She had finished her last year of course work, and her student teaching would be done in two weeks. She hadn't interviewed for a job in twenty years and she was scared to death. She already felt old and dumpy compared to the young coeds in most of her classes. As she went home to cooking and cleaning, they went out to "party" after every class. How could she possibly compete. By the time she had gotten everyone out of bed, fed, and out the door, including their black Labrador, she barely had time to dress and get ready for her interview. By the time she finally found a parking place and the right door to enter the district office, she was already ten minutes late. She was so frazzled she could barely think much less talk intelligently. She felt that her interview already had a poor start.

Teresa Smith was newly divorced and returning to work after twenty years out of the labor force. However, she felt that life was full of challenges, and she was sure she would get through job interviews, as she had managed to land on her feet whenever a new challenge emerged. She had two children at home depending on her, but she had made it clear to them that they needed to contribute to the family by being responsible and getting themselves fed and out the door each morning. The children sometimes complained or hassled each other, but they were good kids and knew when to get it together. She looked at the district office door and knew she was taking an important step toward entering the workforce, and whether or not she was able to land this job, she knew there would be other interviews and her experience interviewing here would make her feel more confident when she took other interviews. She was a bit nervous, but she also knew that she would do her best and had many fine traits to offer this school district, including the maturity to keep things in perspective. As she often reminded herself, "Today is the first day of the rest of my life, and I will make the most of it."

As the Addison School District personnel director, which applicant would you most enjoy opening your office door to? Which one is most likely to come across well in an interview? Both women are very capable, hardworking individuals with a lot to offer Addison School District. However, Linda had already worked herself into a state of panic by the time she entered the personnel director's office. Then, it took her at least fifteen to twenty minutes to get herself to relax.

Due to her fear of failure and her self-doubt, she sets herself up to be even more upset at her next interview as she recalls the negative experience of walking in late and feeling such panic today. Linda needs to pamper herself a little; she needs her family to give her space to think and prepare herself for this special appointment. Her family members are not normally selfish; rather, they are so wrapped up in their lives that they have probably forgotten she has an important interview today. Perhaps, as Teresa did, Linda should have reminded her family last night and arranged for them to meet their own needs as she works toward meeting hers. Individuals who have not had an outside job for many years often find themselves in the position of waiting on others. When a family member's life situation changes, other family members also need to adapt.

After years of going to school, completing a high school diploma, and then finally obtaining a college degree, you probably find it difficult to discover that even though you have completed all the requirements for a teaching certificate you may not automatically obtain a job in your area of expertise. The uncertainty of not knowing if and when you will find a job and where you will need to be located can cause a great deal of stress for you. Most of us like to know we will have a paycheck to depend on. We are also most comfortable when we know what we will be doing in the immediate future. For people who are entering the workforce full-time for the first time in their lives, this may be a particularly upsetting experience as you may not have the background of having successfully obtained a full-time position to help you maintain your self-esteem through the long haul of the typical job search.

For those who are entering the workforce or who are changing careers there may be added responsibilities, such as children to support and college loans to pay off, that further increase your need to secure a paid teaching position. It is most important at this time to remain positive and keep your options open.

However, if you enjoy working with children or adolescents and you enjoyed your student teaching experience, there should be a job out there for you. The key is having the patience and determination to find it and to convince those you will work with that you will be an asset to their educational system.

TIP 1. Always concentrate on the positive.

2. Address any negative in a developmental way; don't dwell on it and get a negative fixation.

Relieving Pressure during the Search

Life today seems to be filled with many types of pressure including stress, inertia, guilt, and feelings of inferiority. It is important to understand the pressures you face and then discover ways to relieve them.

Stress

Remember that stress is a fact of life. It may appear particularly troublesome when you are trying to finish up your education and find a job, but it is a part of life that you have been dealing with, probably quite successfully, for many years. Stress is your body adjusting to changes. It is how you react to these experiences that can create a stress response.

As your brain receives messages of changing events in your environment it makes decisions about how to react. It may decide to ignore the change, or it may decide to set off a reaction of panic and/or anxiety. How you interpret an experience and what you predict for the future can affect how you feel. For example, when you are waiting for a job interview, which in the beginning of your search may be a new experience for you, you can imagine all that can go wrong and tell yourself that you will never get this job or any other job. But, you have the option of telling yourself that no matter how successfully you interview, you will be meeting a new person, learning about a new school district, and getting the opportunity to learn more about interviewing for a teaching position in the future. If you choose to panic and decide that the job interview, or not yet having found a job, is dangerous, your body may react with a stress response that is a signal to the central nervous system to make a series of changes in your body. These body changes, such as increased heart rate and adrenaline secretions, may help you to rapidly run away from danger, but they are not very adaptive when you are looking for the right job. If you feel your body beginning a panic reaction, remember that relaxation is the opposite of stress and that by relaxing your breathing and musculature, you can return your body to its calm state. You do not have to be a victim of your fears. Therefore, the best way to combat these stress reactions is to become aware of their sources and practice relaxing and controlling your impulse to panic. Not only will this be healthier for you, but it will help you be more effective in your search for a job.

TIP   Preparation, preparation, preparation!

---

1. Set your objectives.
2. Develop a time frame.
3. Practice interviewing, review interview questions, and answer questions in depth.
4. Audiotape or videotape yourself interviewing.
    (Being well prepared will build your confidence and help relieve your stress.)

Now try getting yourself jump-started with the Job Hunting Campaign Strategy worksheet designed to keep you on track and motivated (see Figure 8.1.). By having a plan and looking at it daily you will help yourself stay on top of the process.

FIGURE 8.1.   Job Hunting Campaign Strategy Worksheet

Task	Date Begun	Date Completed
• Sign up with a job service		
• Develop resume		
gather credentials		
• Develop multipurpose resume		
• Check for openings		
• Research opening		
district office		
school secretary		
friends		
• Get application		
• Develop job-specific resume		
Remember to stress interview points		
• Write cover letter		
• Fill out application		
• Send in application		
• Interview schedule		
• Follow-up		

Overcoming Inertia

Sometimes life challenges us so much that we feel we are just not up to it and we don't even want to try to compete. When we find ourselves in this frame of mind, it is best to relax and do something to take our mind off our fear and frustration. We can give ourselves permission to postpone our search and then start in again by doing something positive toward our job search as soon as we have cleared our mind. This should not be used as a cop-out, rather to reinforce our decision to get moving and take a necessary step. It is human nature to stall to avoid an unpleasant task; yet we need to rearrange our thinking and jump in and get ourselves going!

Some individuals are so frustrated that they need to allow themselves a break because continuing on is counterproductive. Others find the need to reward themselves only after completing that first task. You must choose what approach works best for you. It might be helpful to write your own personal contract (see Figure 8.2.) This should be done by looking at your job-hunting campaign strategy, discussed earlier in this chapter (Figure 8.1). Remember to reward yourself after setting up dates on the form and in your calendar, and reward yourself along the way as you fill out dates completed. You have succeeded before and now you will do it again.

FIGURE 8.2.   Job Search Contract

After doing something for myself

_____

_____

_____

I will begin Monday at 8:30 with

_____

_____

_____

When I have completed this I will reward myself with
  option 1 _____
  option 2 _____

I will begin with the next step on my chart the next day after my reward.

  signed _____
  date _____
  witness _____

Handling Guilt and Inferiority

There are no rules about how we must feel when it comes to guilt but we have found some interesting differences in guilt between the sexes. In our society, for some reason, individuals who are unemployed often feel guilty about their status and somewhat ashamed, even though the loss of their job may have come through no fault of their own. Often, their guilt and feelings of inferiority are compounded by the fear that they will be unable to provide for their family's needs. This has been especially true for males in our society.

Conversely, individuals in our society (often females) who have stayed home to take care of children—especially those who are just returning to work after a long absence from the employment arena— may feel guilty because they are planning to pursue a career. This guilt stems from leaving their families more on their own, devoting less time to domestic matters, and so on. They worry that they will damage their children psychologically by being away when the children come home from school or by being unavailable to take turns with car pools. Simultaneously, these individuals may worry about the reaction of their spouses, who may be faced with giving up the role of sole provider for the family. Remember, change can be a difficult thing to adjust to, whether it is positive or negative. It is even more difficult if the change is not seen as positive by significant others. If change is difficult for you to handle, think of how the change is also affecting those around you, and hopefully you can practice patience with them. What can you and your significant others do to help smooth the adjustment?

Feelings of guilt and inferiority can best be combated by talking them out honestly and candidly. People reentering the job market may be pleasantly surprised to learn that their friends and families are quite proud of their desire to return to work. Family members can look forward to sharing discussions about their professional days around the dinner table. Similarly, a serious chat with children these days is likely to reveal that many of their friends have two parents working as well and that they don't consider these children deprived in any way. They may well be looking forward to the added comforts that a second salary in the household will provide; they may even be looking forward to exercising more independence than they have previously enjoyed. Consider this a time of learning and growth for all.

People who feel guilty because their lack of employment has limited the family's spending power should likewise be able to talk it over with their spouses and, if they are old enough, the children. They may be amazed to find that family members are sympathetic and that they do not in any way blame them for the temporarily tight budgets. They may be able to make some helpful suggestions for saving money in the interim and may even point out the advantages of this temporary unemployment (the fun of cooking low-cost meals together, getting a chance to see their parent at breakfast or after school, etc.).

Talking with friends and acquaintances who have been in the same situation also helps to alleviate feelings of guilt and inferiority. Talk to a friend who has recently been unemployed and who has subsequently found work. Ask how a family member's temporary loss of salary affected the family; find out how a parent's new job has affected their relationship with their spouse and children. If you feel inferior because of the lack of qualifications or recent experience, talk with someone else who has recently taken a job despite a similar lack of qualifications, and find out how this person is adjusting. Although it is true that misery loves company, it is also a fact that there's nothing like a good success story to give your morale a boost.

Feelings of inferiority can also be alleviated by taking time out to do something you are good at. Spend an evening making a gourmet meal, building something, or teaching a game to the neighborhood kids—anything that gives you a feeling of pride and accomplishment. This feeling of achievement will carry over, helping you to have more confidence in yourself as you search for a job.

Bear in mind that we are usually supersensitive about our own shortcomings. We believe that others are pointing the finger of blame at us when in fact they are doing no such thing. When you were employed, you probably didn't cast aspersions on your unemployed friends; most likely they aren't casting any on you.

Remaining Flexible

Much of the tension of the job search can be alleviated by keeping an open mind about the characteristics that the right job must possess. This does not mean that you should adopt the attitude that any teaching job will do. You must decide just what sort of job you want and then set out with the intention of finding it, as we discussed in an earlier chapter. But at the same time you must avoid setting up such a detailed and rigid list of requirements that the chance of finding such a job is virtually nil.

Flexibility can apply to almost any factor that is prohibiting you from looking favorably on jobs that otherwise suit your specifications. Have you found the perfect job except that it is only for six months of substitute teaching? Take a long look and see if you can't compromise on this one point. Does it really matter as much as you think it does? Perhaps you can afford to take a substitute job as you wait for a full-time job to open up in this nearby district.

The issue of relocation can also create a great deal of stress, and flexibility may be necessary here. If you are in a distressed labor market, face up to the relocation question early and consider looking by choice in an area where teaching jobs are more abundant, rather than grimly holding on until you are forced to relocate. Try not to let climate become your only consideration when relocating. Many areas with ideal climates have loaded employment markets or low-paying job opportunities simply because so many people like living and working there. By all means, if you wish to live in a particular spot, look for a job there—but don't make this such a rigid requirement that you suffer mental anguish and the inability to search elsewhere if the job you want doesn't turn up.

Adopting an Optimistic Outlook

In all phases of the job search, try to replace negative feelings and motivations with positive ones. This sort of optimism can go a long way toward helping you accept minor irritations and defeats philosophically instead of letting them get you down psychologically.

For instance, let's look again at Linda. If she has the attitude that says, "I have to go to work full-time whether I want to or not, to help pay for the children's education and to meet the high interest rates on the mortgage," her entire viewpoint about the job search may be pessimistic or negative. These may be very legitimate reasons for her return to work, but if they are the only reasons she has explored, she may well approach the task with a negative mental set and with a certain amount of resentment. The same woman, with the help of a little positive thinking, could tell herself: "The children will all be off at college soon, and there probably won't be as much to do around the home. I probably wouldn't be satisfied with just joining a class to fill my time. It's time I started planning for my own future and growth. Wouldn't it be challenging to return to work to see if I can contribute in a different way? I can grow personally, recapture some of my old abilities, and add new skills that will provide me with a feeling of accomplishment and self-satisfaction. I loved having the opportunity to be at home with the kids but now I think I will enjoy working in the schools. Maybe a new, dynamic environment will be invigorating. Sounds exciting! I'll start by establishing some new personal goals for the next six months, including finding a job that's challenging and fun."

The applicant who has adopted the optimistic viewpoint is going to be better prepared to seek out and evaluate job opportunities and to end up with a position that has the greatest potential for personal fulfillment.

Seeking Creative Solutions

In almost every job search, there comes a time when applicants must decide what is bothering them and take steps to remedy the situation. Anything that creates doubts, worry, stress, or depression qualifies as deserving a creative solution. Otherwise, the disturbance will bother you until you become ineffective in your job search and show a lack of self-confidence in your interviews. If you are nervous about your appearance during interviews, do something about it! Invest in a new suit or ask a friend to survey your wardrobe and help you decide what to wear. If you feel your skills are too rusty, enroll in a class or take a teaching workshop. If you have been away from teaching for a while, read up on what's new in the field. Alleviate worries by holding a family meeting and redistributing tasks so that everybody pitches in. In order to lighten the financial burden until you find a job, take out a loan or talk with your creditors about the possibility of delaying payments until you have started working again. Once you have taken steps to solve these worries, whether they are large or small, your mind will be free to concentrate on the task at hand and your entire attitude toward job hunting will improve.

TIP   No one likes rejections, however you can:

1.   Buffer a rejection with a positive activity and an upbeat approach. (Do a positive critique.)
2.   Regard any rejection as a learning experience and then put it behind you.

Coping with Rejections

In many parts of the country, there is great competition for jobs in education. Almost inevitably, a job candidate will encounter rejections before finally being offered a position he or she wants. All too often, rejection acts as a shattering blow to the ego. People who are turned down may see themselves as failures, become frustrated, and stop trying.

It helps sometimes to put your own rejection in perspective by looking at the average length of time it takes others in your area to get a job. The more experience you have, normally, the more money a district will have to pay you, making it tougher to find a job.

Obviously, anyone who has searched for employment has encountered rejections along the way. And presumably the right job—or at least an acceptable job—has turned up in the end. This knowledge may not make your own rejection any easier to swallow at the time, but it does indicate that you are not the only applicant who has ever been turned down. There is certainly no reason to give up in despair or feel hopeless just because the first interview, or even the first month of interviews, ends up in rejection. Instead remember, many school districts don't know in March what positions will need to be filled August 29.

Why Teachers Are Turned Down

Before you become too depressed over a rejection, try to remind yourself that there are many reasons for rejecting an applicant—some of them valid, some of them not so reasonable. A rejection does not necessarily mean that you were not considered suitable for the job. It is quite possible that you were the very best candidate, in terms of qualifications and experience, but that someone almost as well qualified scored higher on a particular test, happened to be the boss's nephew, had a recommendation from a more influential person, or had no experience so would do the same job for a lot less money. Maybe it was a toss-up between you and another applicant, and the other person got the job because they happen to share a love of skydiving with the individual who made the hiring decision. Maybe extra points were awarded to the second-ranked candidate for agreeing to coach the debate team, and those few extra points were enough to allow him or her to edge you out of the top spot.

In cases where you know you were in the running until the final job offer was made, rejection is a bitter pill to swallow, but it is not a cause for despair or anger. Get a firm hold on your emotions and don't panic. If you were one of the top candidates out of a field of many, that's encouraging; try to consider it a compliment to your credentials that you made it to one of the finalist spots and take new hope that you will be the top candidate next time around.

Many candidates are also rejected who were never seriously in the running for the job, either because they were underqualified or inexperienced or because they did not make a favorable impression during the interviews.

Viewing Rejection as a Learning Experience

Rejection by a prospective employer can provide a profitable learning experience for the candidate who is mature enough to look at the situation analytically. The first step is to try to determine why, specifically, another applicant was offered the job instead of you. If the opportunity arises, ask the interviewer why you were turned down when you are called and told that this is the case. If it is a simple matter of a lack of certification or experience, you will probably get a straightforward answer. This is valuable information; perhaps you need to sell yourself in a different way.

If you were adequately qualified (and you can generally assume that you were, if you were interviewed in depth or called back for more than one interview before being turned down), this is also valuable information because it lets you assume that if you keep trying for the same general sort of teaching position, you will eventually receive an employment offer.

If you have no clue about how your qualifications stacked up or if you believe that something other than your work-related qualifications kept you from receiving an offer, review your interview. Was there anything in your appearance, manner, or behavior that could have worked against you? How did you feel about your performance during the interview and about the relationship you established with the interviewer? If you felt awkward or less than confident during the interview or if you were unable to answer some of the questions posed, perhaps you need to spend a little time practicing your interviewing skills or boning up on the specific field in which you are seeking employment. Even if you never figure out why you were rejected, the experience of being interviewed and turned down was not in vain if it gave you practice, thus improving your technique and bolstering your confidence for the next time around.

The Chances for Reconsideration

If you are rejected for a particular opening in a district you hoped to work for, don't ruin future chances by acting angry, hurt, or immature. By displaying the right attitude, you may be keeping your options open and your name under consideration. If the principal calls to tell you they have offered the job to someone else, thank him or her for letting you know and ask whether you were missing any of the qualifications they were looking for. Say that you appreciated the chance to interview with them, that you were very impressed with what you saw of the school, and that you especially enjoyed talking with your contact there. Make it clear that you would like to be considered for any other suitable job openings that may come up elsewhere in the district, and ask whether there is anyone else you should get in touch with to express this interest. If you are rejected by letter rather than by phone, take the time to write back, expressing the above sentiments.

This may seem like a lot of work for nothing, especially if your first reaction to rejection is anger or resentment. In many cases, however, the little extra effort has proved to be worth a job. Once in a while applicant number one doesn't work out, and applicant number two (possibly you) is called with a job offer an amazingly short time later. Even more often, an opening may turn up later. The principal or personnel director will remember bright, polite applicant number two (you again), who would be perfect for the new opening. Thus, by taking a few minutes to follow through in a mature manner after being turned down, you may find yourself a perfect job after all.

Reevaluating and Continuing the Search

In summary, then, a turndown is not a major setback in your job search unless your own attitude makes it one. Indeed, rejections can actually help you in the long run by providing the fuel for reevaluation of your credentials and goals and by lending insight into the interviewing process that may stand you in good stead when the right job comes along. Wise candidates will learn all they can from rejections, refuse to become discouraged, revise their resumes and/or their portfolios if necessary, and go right on searching for that perfect job. Happy Hunting!

BIBLIOGRAPHY

American Association for Employment in Education. (1992). "Characteristics That School Systems Value." *The Job Service Handbook*. Evanston, IL: Charles Marshall.

Educational Testing Service. (1998). *System of Interactive Guidance and Information Plus Program*. Princeton, NJ: Educational Testing Service.

Gallup Organization. *SRA Teacher Perceiver*. Lincoln, NE: Gallup Organization.

Harmon, L.W., J. C. Hansen, F. H. Borgen, and A. L. Hammer. (1994). *Strong Interest Inventory: Applications and Technical Guide*. Palo Alto, CA: Consulting Psychologists Press, 377–383.

Moffatt, T. L. (1987). *Land That Job*. Madison, WI: Science Tech Publishers.

University of Wisconsin–Madison Educational Placement and Career Services. University of Wisconsin–Madison, Madison, WI.

Yates, M. (1997). *Knock 'Em Dead*. Holbrook, MA: Adams Media Corporation.

INDEX